CRICUT MAKER

THE ESSENTIAL GUIDE FOR BEGINNERS TO USE THEIR CRICUT MAKER

Made with love

by

Sienna

Tally

Table of Contents

Introduction

First of all, thank you for purchasing this "Cricut Maker" guide. As you can understand from the name, this book is not dedicated to understanding and using a specific Cricut model (for more information about this, you can visit my bibliography, where you can find other guides explicitly created for each model of Cricut released until today!) In this guide, it doesn't matter if you are an expert in crafting or just starting. We will start enriching your skills and your cultural background together. In the year 2017, a new model in the Cricut family was released called The Cricut Maker™. This has all the bells and whistles to do most anything. It can cut more materials than any previous models, and the company boasts its fast, precise cutting.

The Cricut Maker is considered to be Cricut's flagship model. This is the one that can do just about anything under the sun on just about any material you can fit into the mat guides of your machine. The one drawback of this powerhouse model is the price point. This does make this model more prohibitive unless you plan to create crafts that you can sell with this model. If this is your intention, you can rest assured that whatever you turn out with this machine will be the best of the best, every single time. If you're selling your crafts, this baby will pay for itself in little to no time at all.

With that in mind, the Cricut Maker costs $399.99. That is a large sum of money for someone who doesn't have it and even someone who does have it. Although there's a lot you can do with $399.99, there are just as many things you can do with the Cricut Maker. My advice would be to save until you can afford it or put it on your wishlist in the meantime and subtly hint to your loved ones that you'll love to have one of these bad boys. Hopefully, someone will catch on and not balk at the massive amount of dollars that it will eat up.

The Cricut Maker can be used with your images, a plus for those who prefer to use their own or don't want to buy a subscription or pay for individual photos. It allows you to personalize your items and make your statement. You can create personalized cards, signs, and anything your heart desires. The ability to personalize your items with multiple lines and fonts broadens your horizon, and if you make products to sell, you can offer personalization.

Chapter 1
What Is a Cricut Maker Machine

CRICUT MAKER

This is another model of the Cricut machine. This model is considered among the top-ranking Cricut machines and is used for more demanding and professional DIY tasks and performances. Suited to take on materials of up to 12 inches in width, the Cricut Maker can cut up to 300 and above materials, including the more-difficult-to-cut materials like wood. The Cricut Maker has a high durability level. Considering the usability of this machine is easy to be learned, following the guide which the Cricut machines come with or with explainer content scattered across the internet.

The Cricut Maker has a wide range of adaptability as it can be used for a host of tasks, including cutting, writing, scoring. Other professional effects need a more complex machine that possesses extra features. This model of the devices comes with a double tool holder and can perform tasks at a rate that is faster when compared to other Cricut machines; up to 2 times as fast. The Cricut Maker supports the print and cuts feature, which allows the user of the device to get more

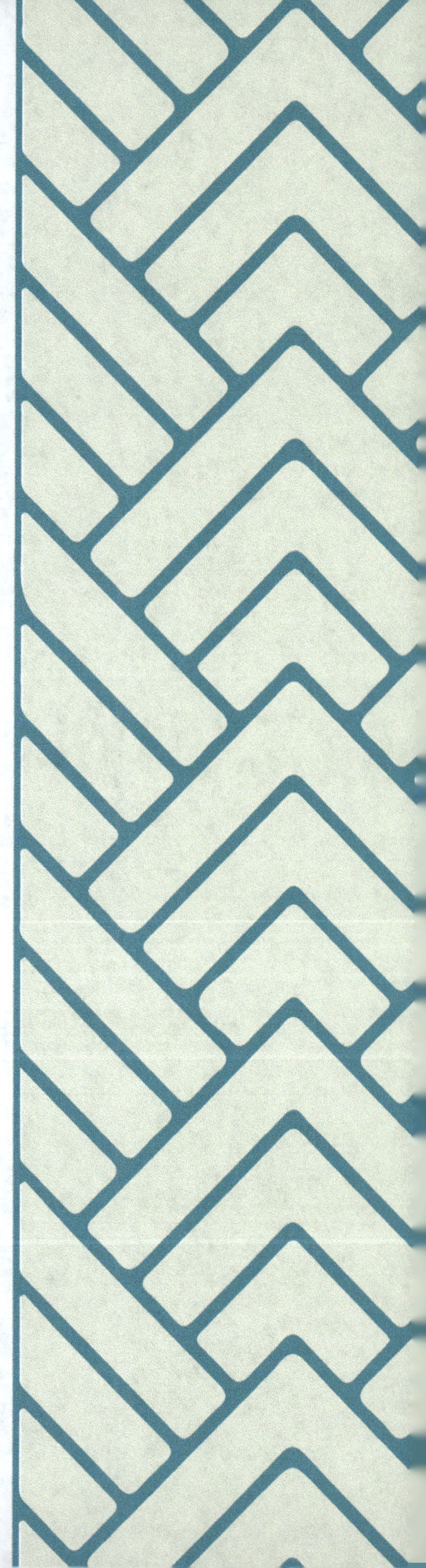

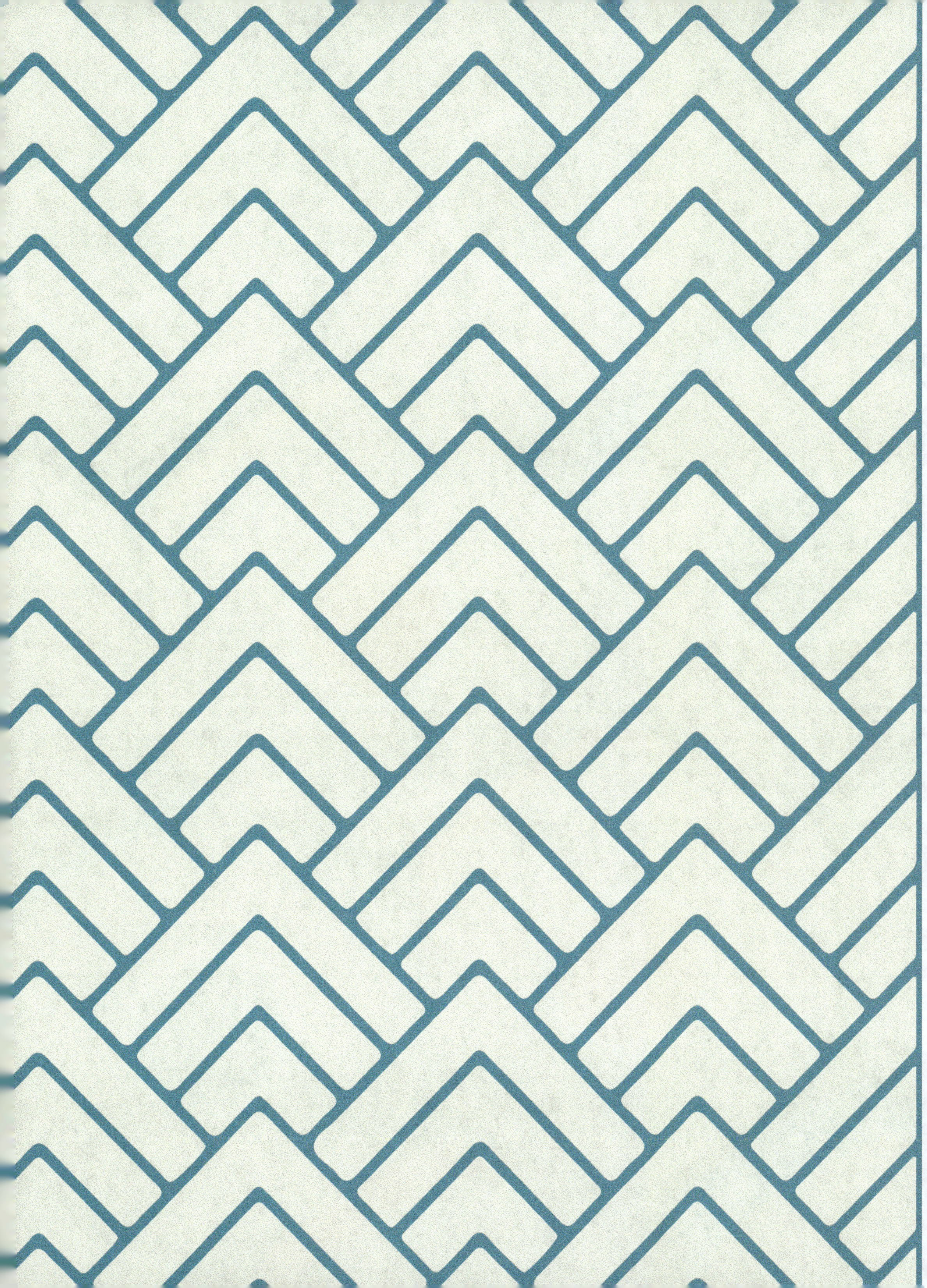

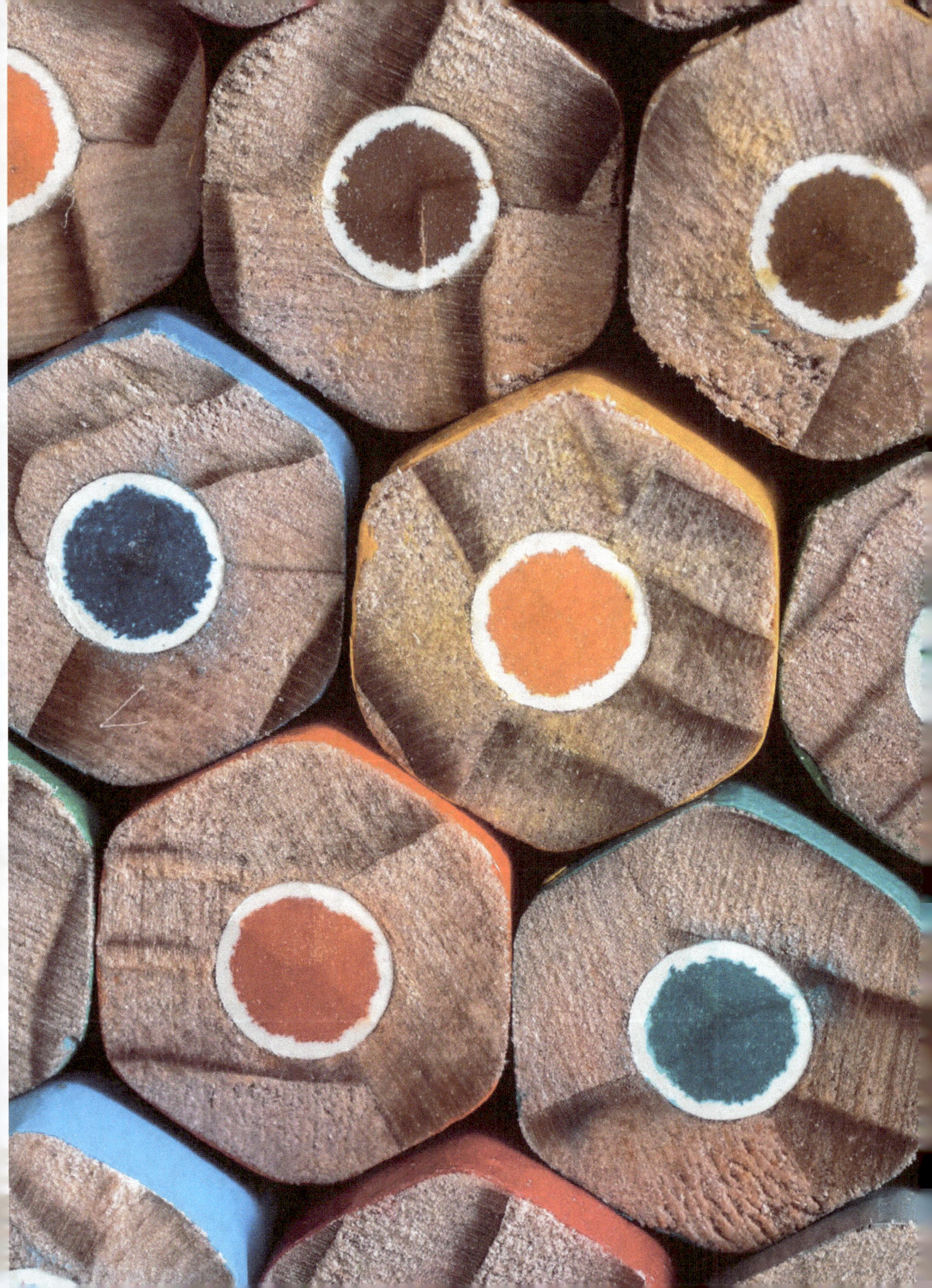

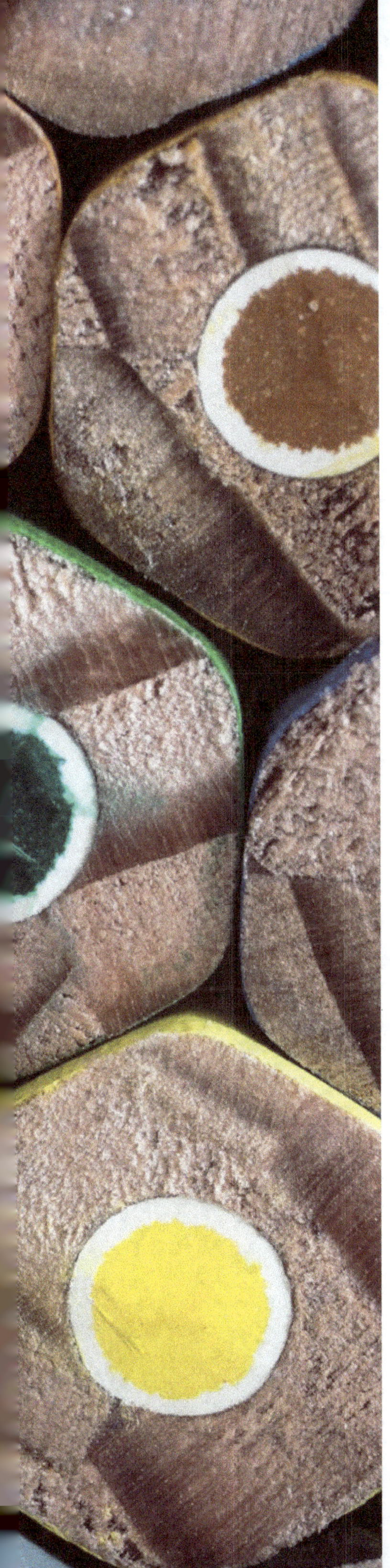

creative with the tasks at hand and opens up the doors to a wide range of craft opportunities. The Cricut Maker is ten times more potent than other Cricut machines and can make many designs and DIY crafts.

Just like the others, it is operated by connecting it to the design space application that is free and available on the iOS, Android, Windows, and Mac platforms. The machine and the powering device can be established wirelessly, using the Bluetooth connection, or using the USB cord as provided alongside the machine.

Summary:

- Holds 12″ x 24″ or 12″ x 12″ mat
- Uses cable or Bluetooth to connect to Cricut Design Space
- Has Bluetooth technology
- Requires internet and software
- Cuts SVG images
  - It cuts any font from your computer
- Print your design to your printer and cuts it out with the Cricut Maker later
  - Has dual carriage
- Uses rotary blade

PROS

It has a rotary blade. What does that mean, you ask? Well, let me tell you that it means there will be no more material for you to cut by hand. The rotary blade can slice through virtually any fabric, from silk to denim to canvas. Not only does that cancel out any hand-cutting incident, but it also guarantees that you won't need another machine to do the large-scale projects either!

The blade can cut through materials that are less than 2.5-mm thick. With the new Knife Blade on the playing field now, the entire game is changed! Aside from penetrating thicker and tougher items, its lifespan is also significantly longer than any other tool. It saves you money in the long run, as well as the hassle of purchasing more blades. It's just overall better than any of its counterparts.

You know that time when you contemplate buying another iPhone, but you know the next one will be around as soon as you purchase it, then you're stuck with the old one, and the cycle just repeats itself? That won't happen with the Cricut Maker. Do you know why? It is because Cricut came up with the brilliant idea that not only makes the Cricut Maker compatible with all of the current Cricut products but also with every Cricut merchandise to come! This means that you will only have to buy the tools instead of getting new machines with new features. This investment looks better and better with every word, doesn't it?

Storage and holders. I am a big fan of any form of container, storage unit, or anything I can use to organize things. Luckily, the Cricut Maker has those! There is a space on the machine to support whatever device you are using to keep your design in front of you as you work at all times. Not only that, but there are a drawer and a couple of tool cups. One of which is lined with rubber, so it doesn't damage your blades when you store them in there. Isn't that nifty? It is excellent to keep all of your instruments in one place, and the Cricut Maker has more than enough space for any additional items

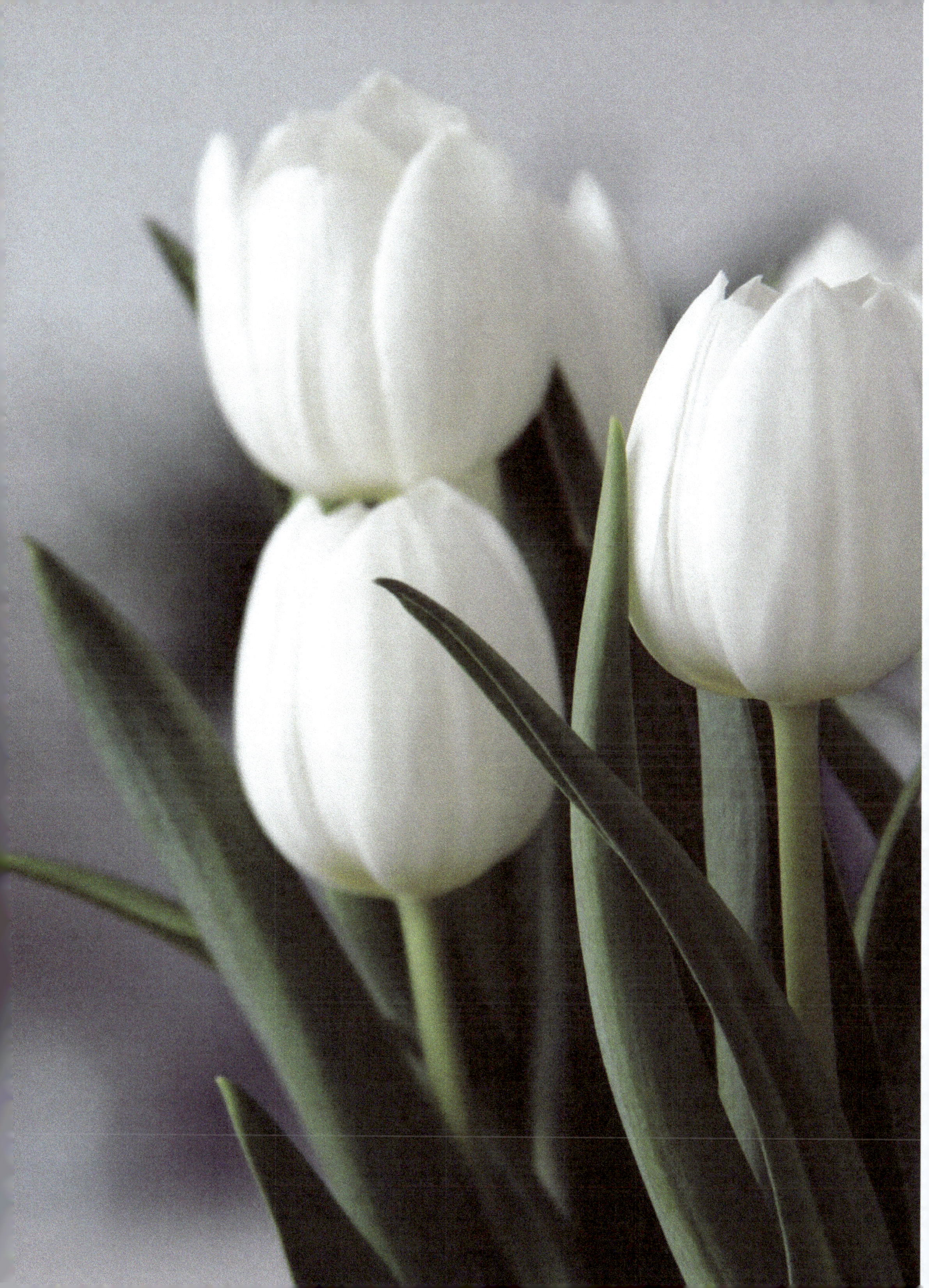

that you decide to purchase alongside it.

It gives you access to an extensive sewing pattern library. Even to someone like me who hates sewing, this is exciting. It makes me want to give it another go. I'm just waiting for Cricut to make a sewing machine first.

Price

You are probably waiting for this giant ball to drop, aren't you? Well, before I tell you how much this machine costs, remember that Cricut Maker is a machine for life, considering it will work with any tool Cricut releases in the future. It is beautiful and powerful as heck.

With that in mind, the Cricut Maker costs $399.99. That is a large sum of money for someone who doesn't have it and even someone who does have it. Although there's a lot you can do with $399.99, there are just as many things you can do with the Cricut Maker. My advice would be to save until you can afford it or put it on your wishlist in the meantime and subtly hint to your loved ones that you'll love to have one of these bad boys. Hopefully, someone will catch on and not balk at the massive amount of dollars that it will eat up.

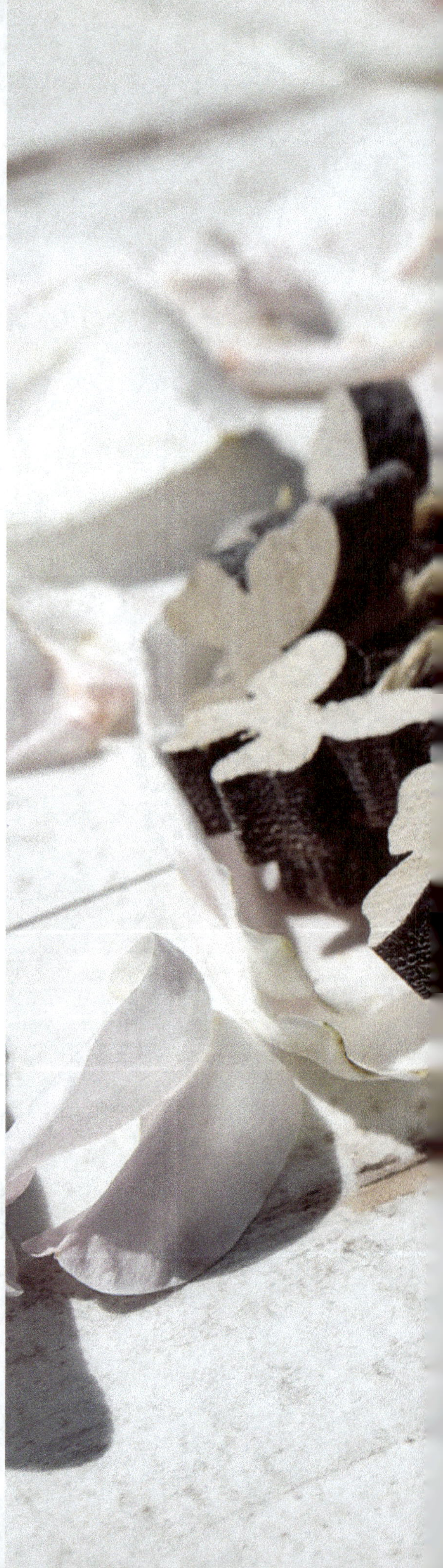

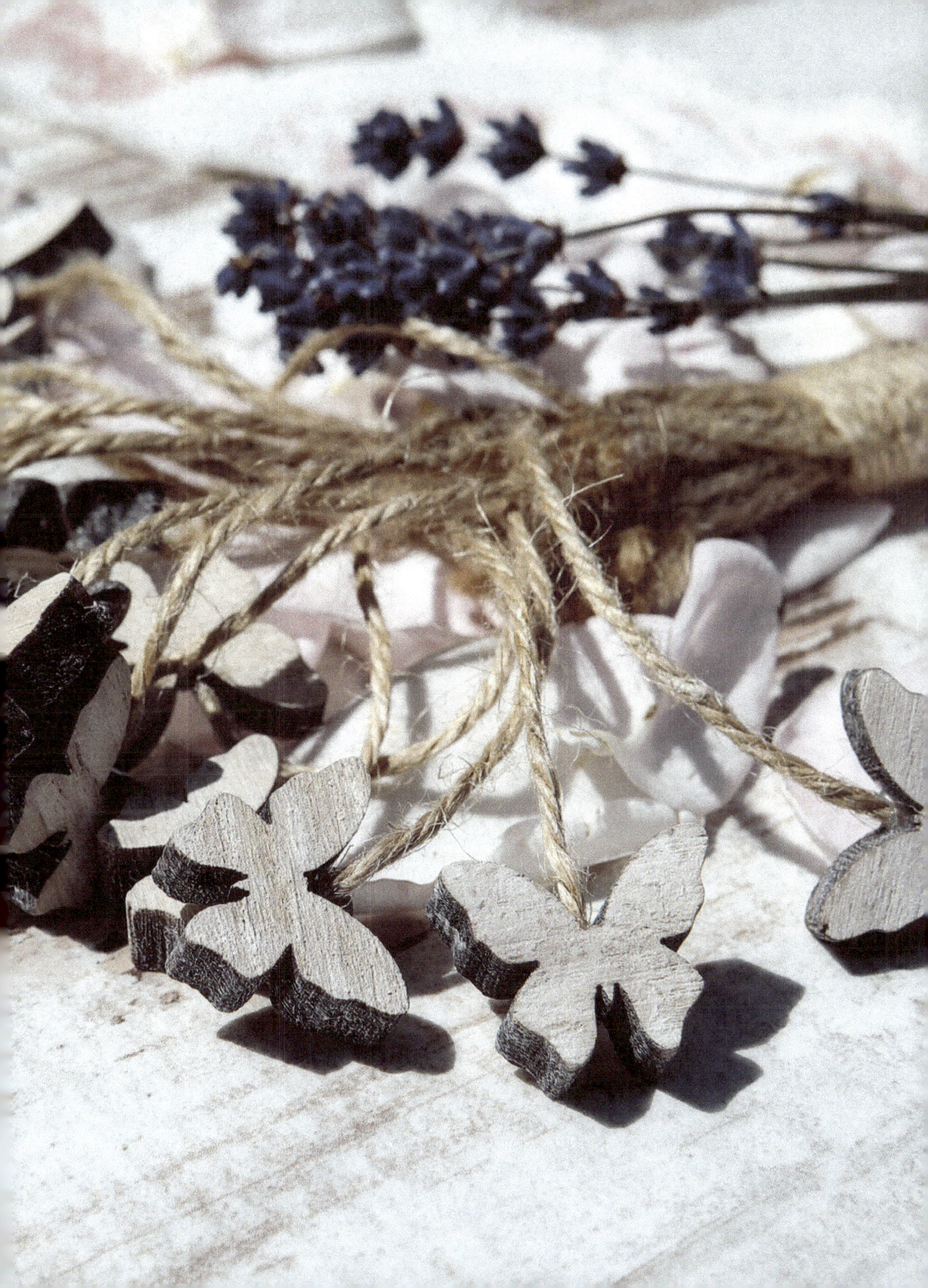

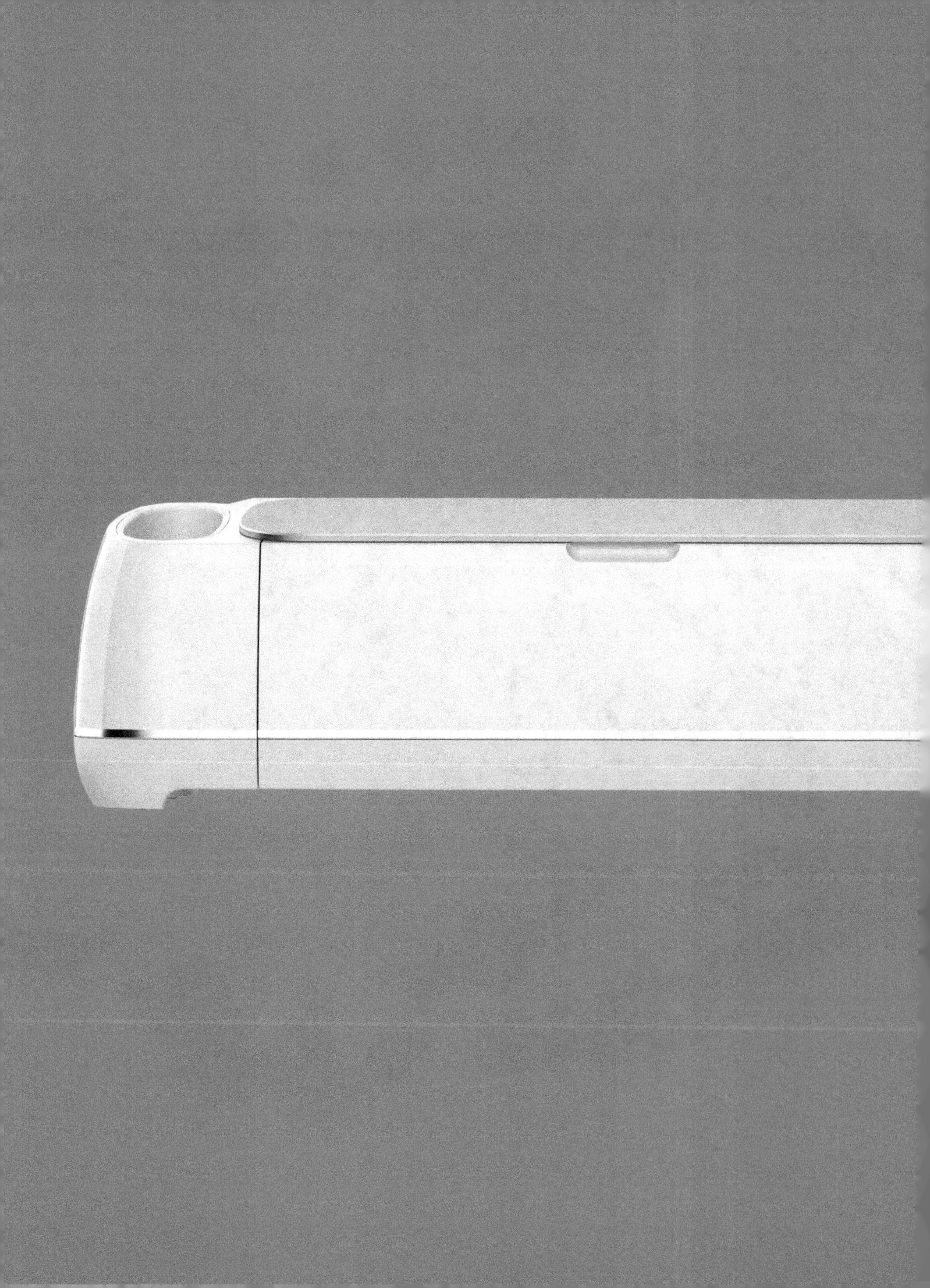

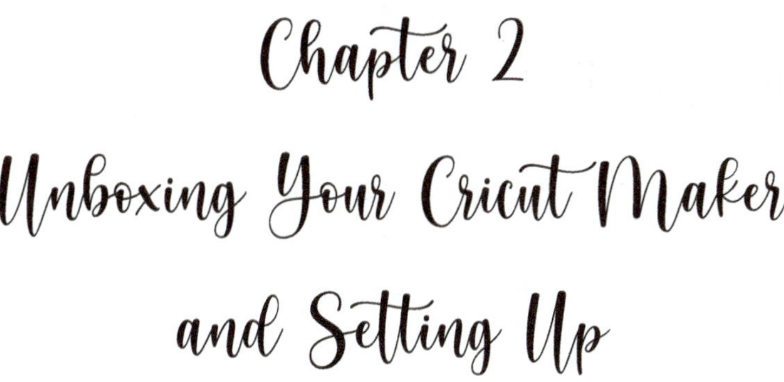

Chapter 2
Unboxing Your Cricut Maker and Setting Up

The Cricut Maker is a beautiful craft cutting machine that does open up new crafting possibilities. You can get debossing blade tips, engraving blade tips, and a cutting knife that can cut materials such as wood. It does need a bit of space as it is a standard-sized craft cutting machine much the same size as the preceding Cricut missing machine models.

Open the Top Flap

To open the Cricut Maker, flip up the top flap, which automatically opens up the machine's front door.

CRICUT MAKER MACHINE TOP, FRONT, AND INSIDE OVERVIEW

The following overview of the machine starts with the machine's front from the left-hand side when sitting in front of the cutting machine.

TOOL CUPS

There is a dual-slot for crafting tools such as a pair of scissors, tweezers, weeding tools, and so on on the machine's left-hand side. It has one pocket more in-depth than the other, each with a protective silicone base for any blades that may be stored.

MOBILE DEVICE HOLDER SLOT

Beneath the machine's top flap, there is a long groove that runs over the mouth of the cutting machine. This slot is conveniently designed to hold a mobile device such as a phone or tablet.

CRICUT CARTRIDGE PORT

The Cricut Maker machine does not come with a Cricut Cartridge port, but it can still take cartridges with the help of a USB cartridge adaptor sold separately.

TOP LID

The top lid flips up and offers support for a mobile phone or tablet to lean against if they are inserted into the mobile device slot. It is also a protective cover for the machine when it is not in use.

CRICUT ACCESSORY AND BLADE HOUSING HEAD

In the mouth of the machine, you will find the Cricut accessory and blade housing head. This head holds the accessory and blade clamps. This housing is a double tool holder, making it easier for the machine to operate dual functions such as cutting and scoring simultaneously. This means that you do not have to change accessories halfway through a project.
This housing head moves along a housing head guide bar located a little way back from, but just above, the material feeder guide bar.

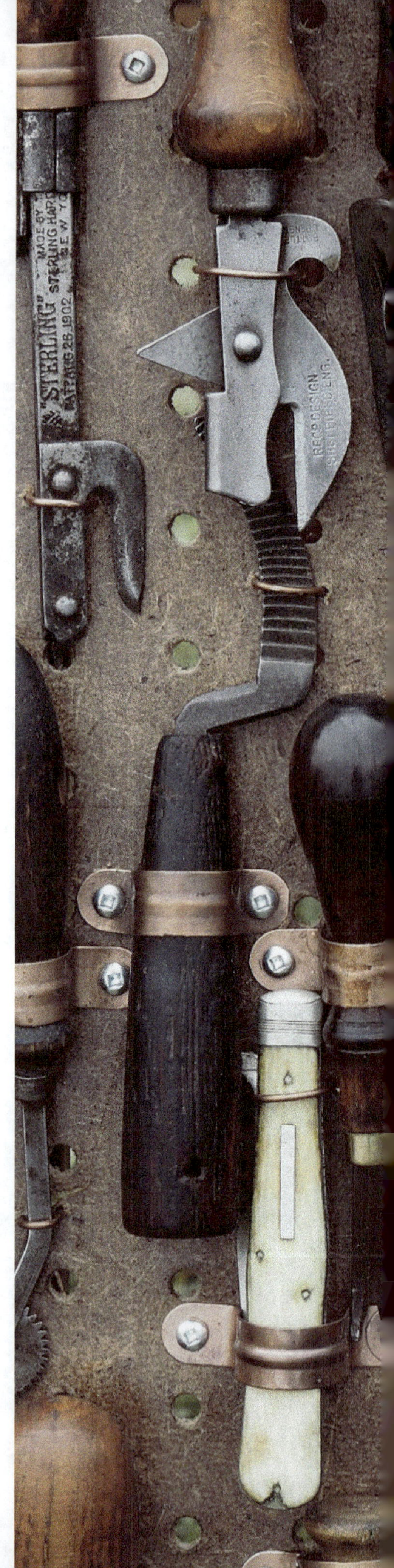

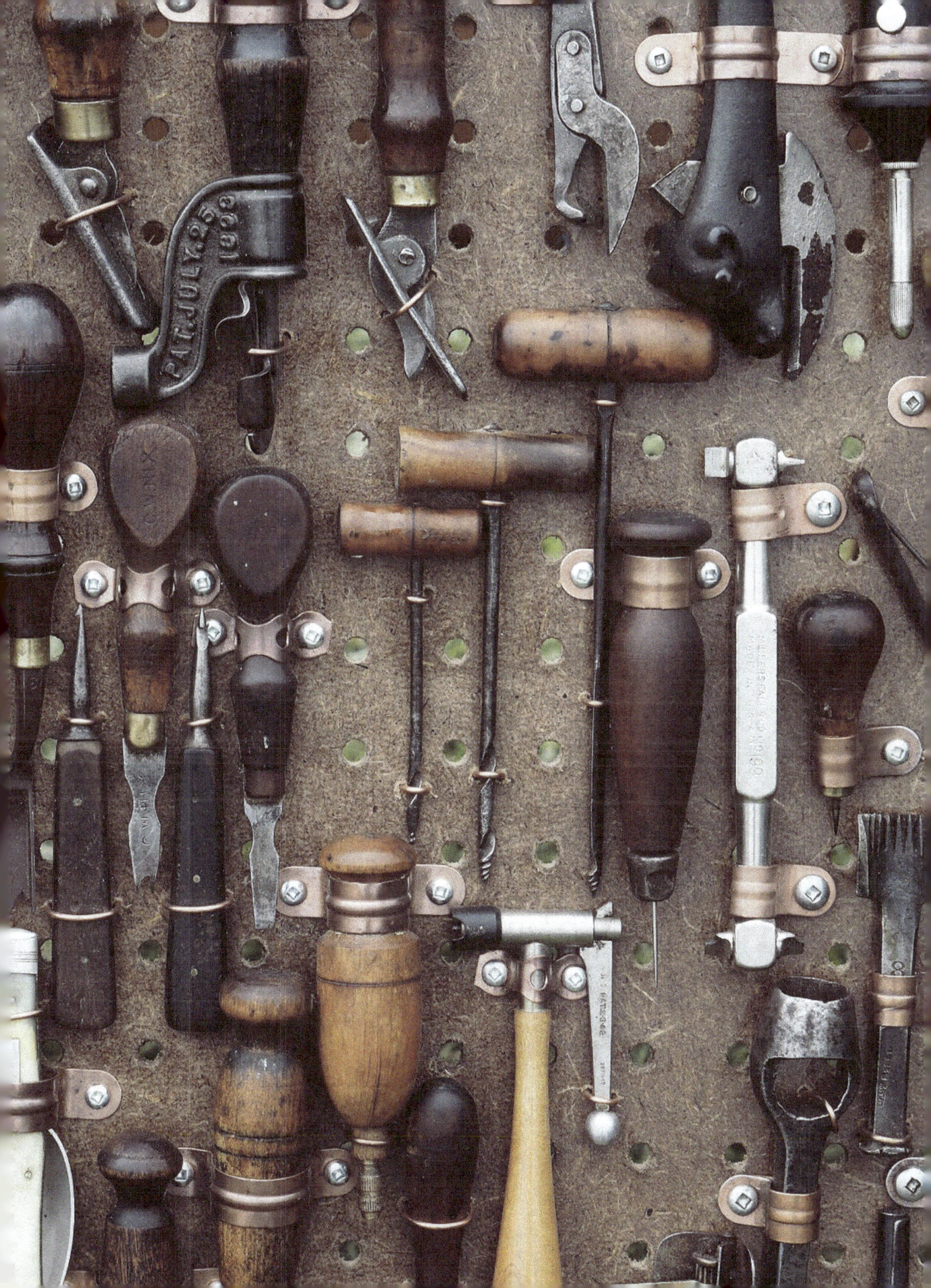

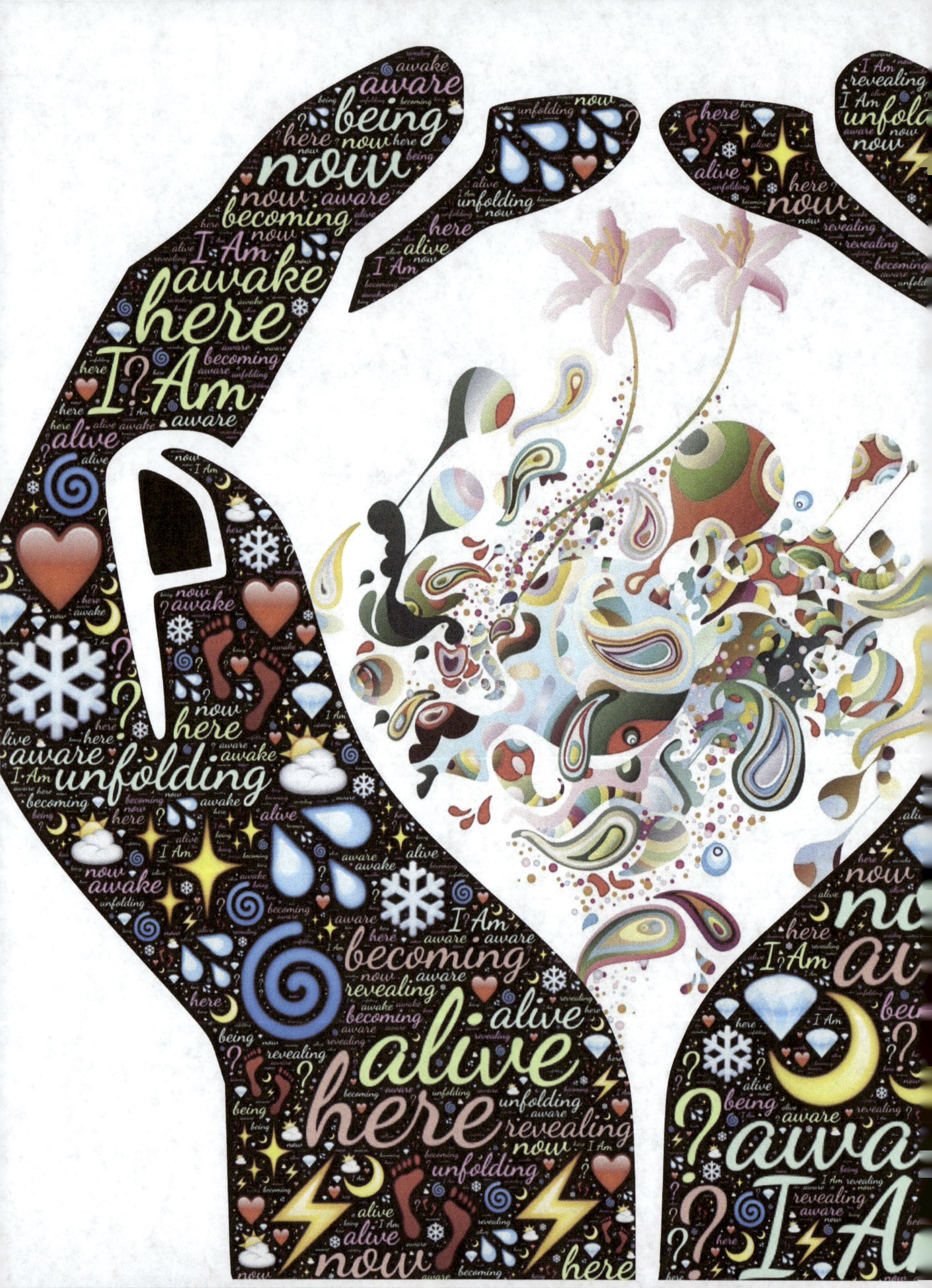

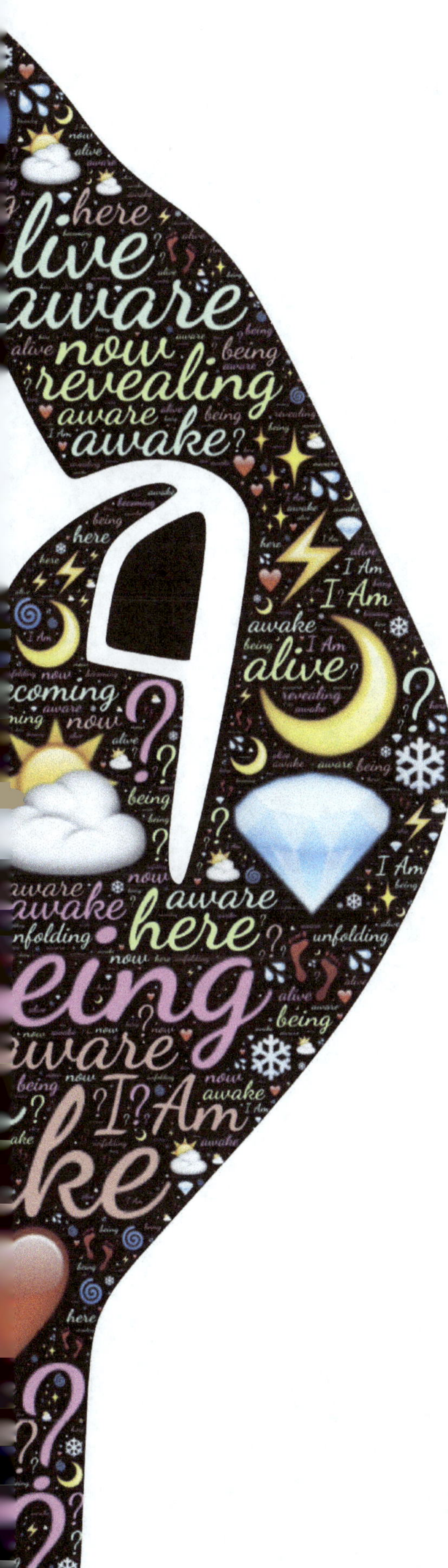

ACCESSORY CLAMP A

Accessory clamp A is for the Scoring Stylus pen and other Cricut drawing or marking pens compatible with the cutting machine.

BLADE CLAMP B

Blade clamp B is for blades and blade housings.
Material Feeder Guide Bar
The material feeder guide bar helps to hold the cutting mat steady so that the cutting blades can glide over the material.

FEEDER GUIDE ROLLERS

The feeder guide rollers are the two grey rollers located on either side of the material feeder guide bar. These rollers roll the material back and forth so that the machine can cut the materials.

STAR WHEELS

The star wheels are the small, white wheels that look like little stars. There are four of them, and they are located between the two grey feeder guide rollers. They help to keep the material steady during cutting. Some materials will require moving these little wheels to the one side of the bar not to make indents in the material. Some material is too thick for these small wheels and could cause them damage.

MAT GUIDES

These are the two little plastic feet that are located in front of the gray feeder guide rollers. They guide the cutting mats into position and mark the full cutting mat or material size fed through the cutting machine.

BOTTOM FEEDER PLATE

The bottom feeder plate is the portion that the material will sit on while it is being cut and will rest upon when the cut is finished. The plate also

BOTTOM STORAGE DRAWER

The bottom storage drawer is a secret compartment that is housed in the bottom feeder plate. Here, you can store your accessories such as cutting rulers, pins, scissors, scraper, drive housings, and so on. There is a long compartment, a smaller square compartment, and two smaller ones. One of the smaller bins contains a significant magnetic stipend for keeping blades and pins from rattling around the room.

LOAD/UNLOAD MAT BUTTON

On the top right-hand side of the machine, the front, is the load/unload cutting mat button. This button has an up and down arrow on it to indicate load and unload. This is the button you will use to load the cutting into the machine when you are ready to cut. It is also the button that

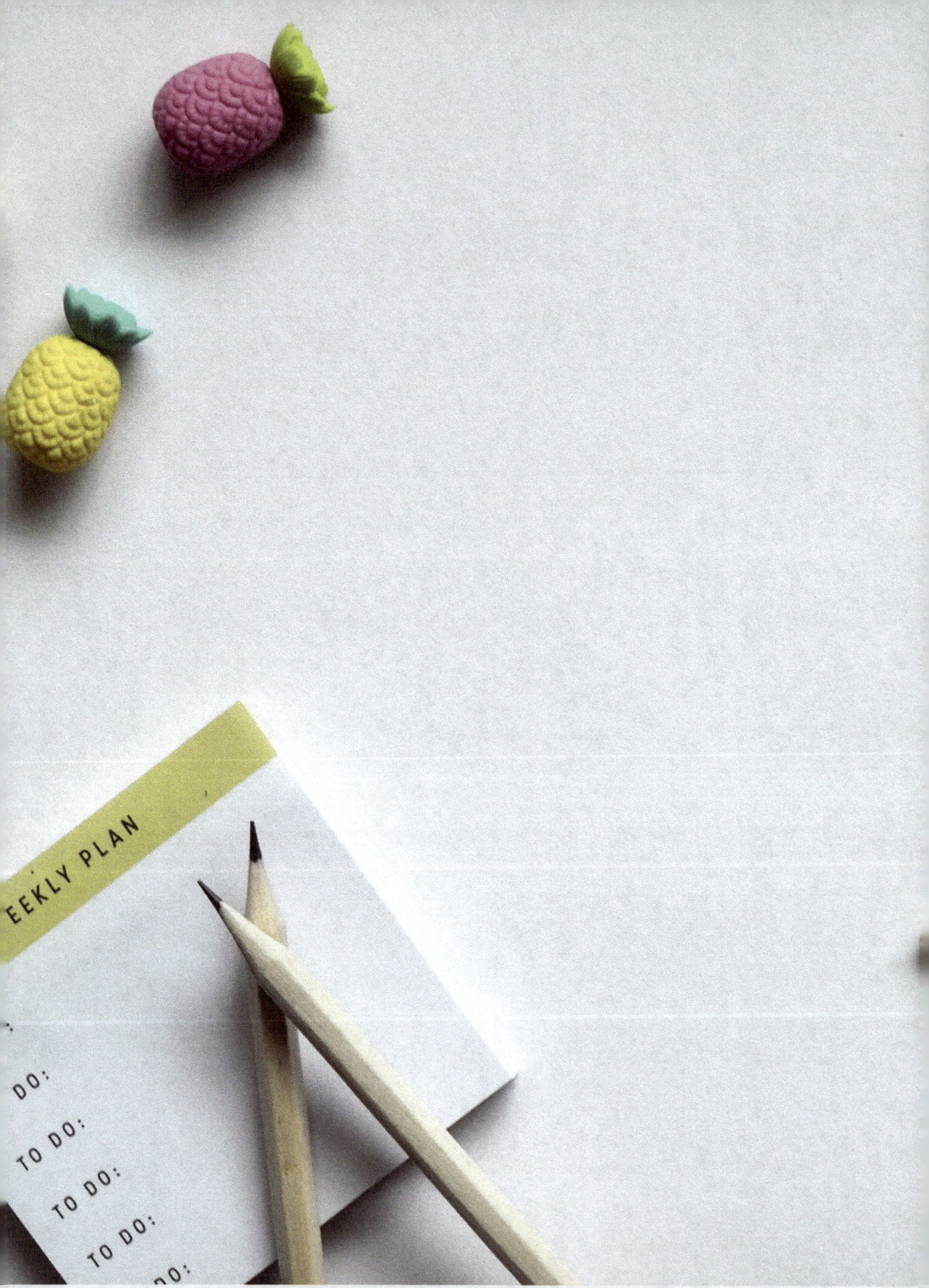
EEKLY PLAN
DO:
TO DO:
TO DO:
TO DO:
TO DO:

you will use to unload the cutting mat once the cutting device has finished cutting the design.

GO BUTTON

The Go button is located right next to the load/unload cutting mat button and is marked with a little green "C" for Cricut. This is the button that you will press when you are ready to start cutting the design.

PAUSE BUTTON

At times, you may need to stop cutting for whatever reason. This is when this button comes in handy. It is located next to the go button and is marked with two lines running next to each other, much like the pause button on any electronic gaming, TV, or DVD device.

SMART SET DIAL

The Cricut Maker does not have a Smart Set dial. The material selection is chosen through the Design Space software.

POWER BUTTON

The power button is located just above the load/unload cutting mat button on the cutting machine's top.

USB UTILITY PORT

The USB utility port is located at the bottom right-hand side of the machine. This port is used to charge mobile devices while connected via Bluetooth to the engine for cutting. It must not be confused with the USB port at the back of the machine, which is used to connect the device to a computer.

USB PORT

The USB port for the machine is located at the back of the engine near the power port. This is used to update the machine's firmware and to connect to a device.

POWER PORT

The Cricut Maker's power port is located at the back of the cutting machine.

MATERIAL FEEDER SLOT

The cutter cuts materials up to 12" long at one time. The edge needs to slide the mat back and forth across the blade or any accessories loaded for the project to cut out these patterns.
That is why there is a material feeder slot at the back of the machine; so the mat can slide in and out to cut the material's full length.

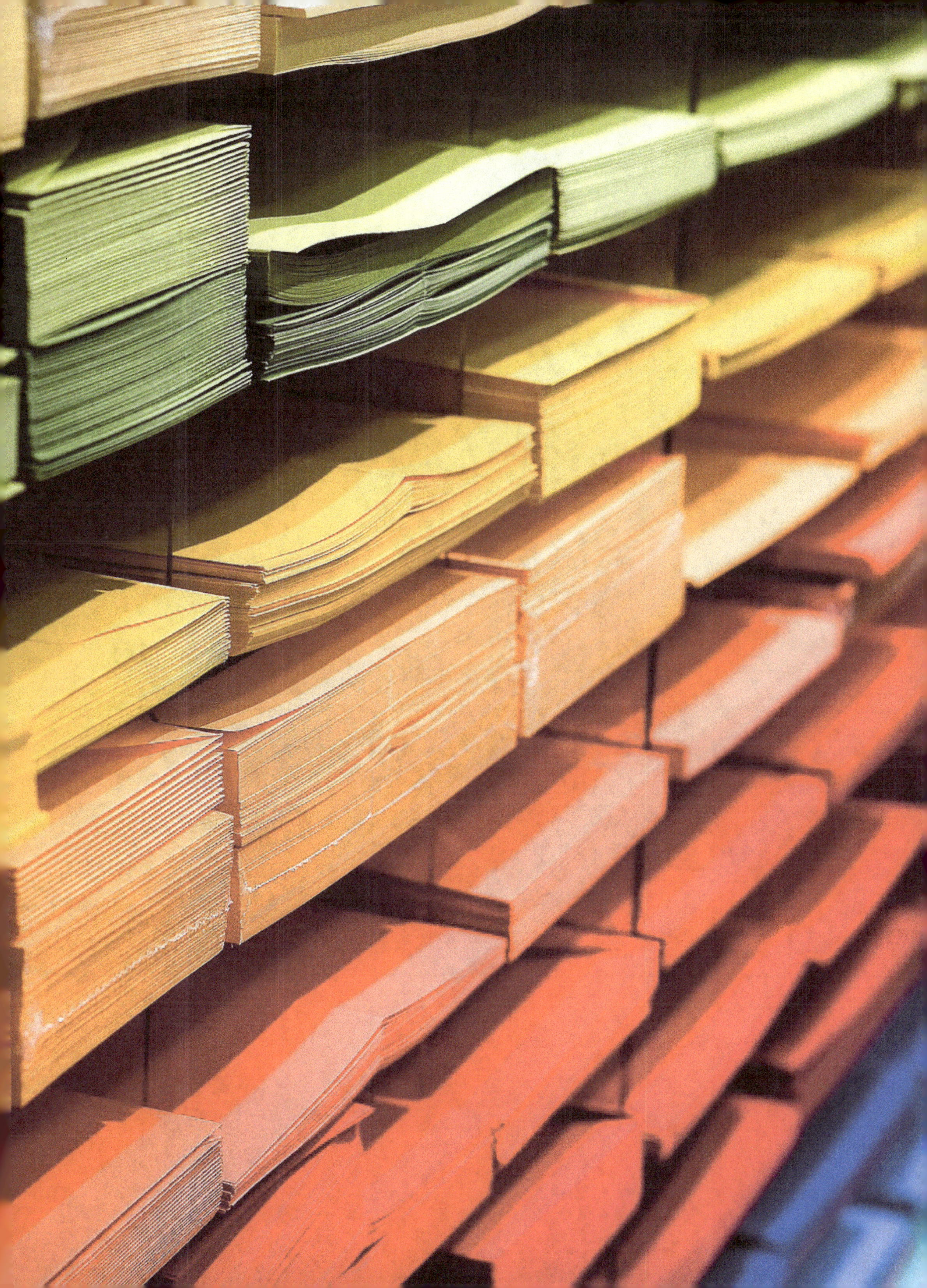

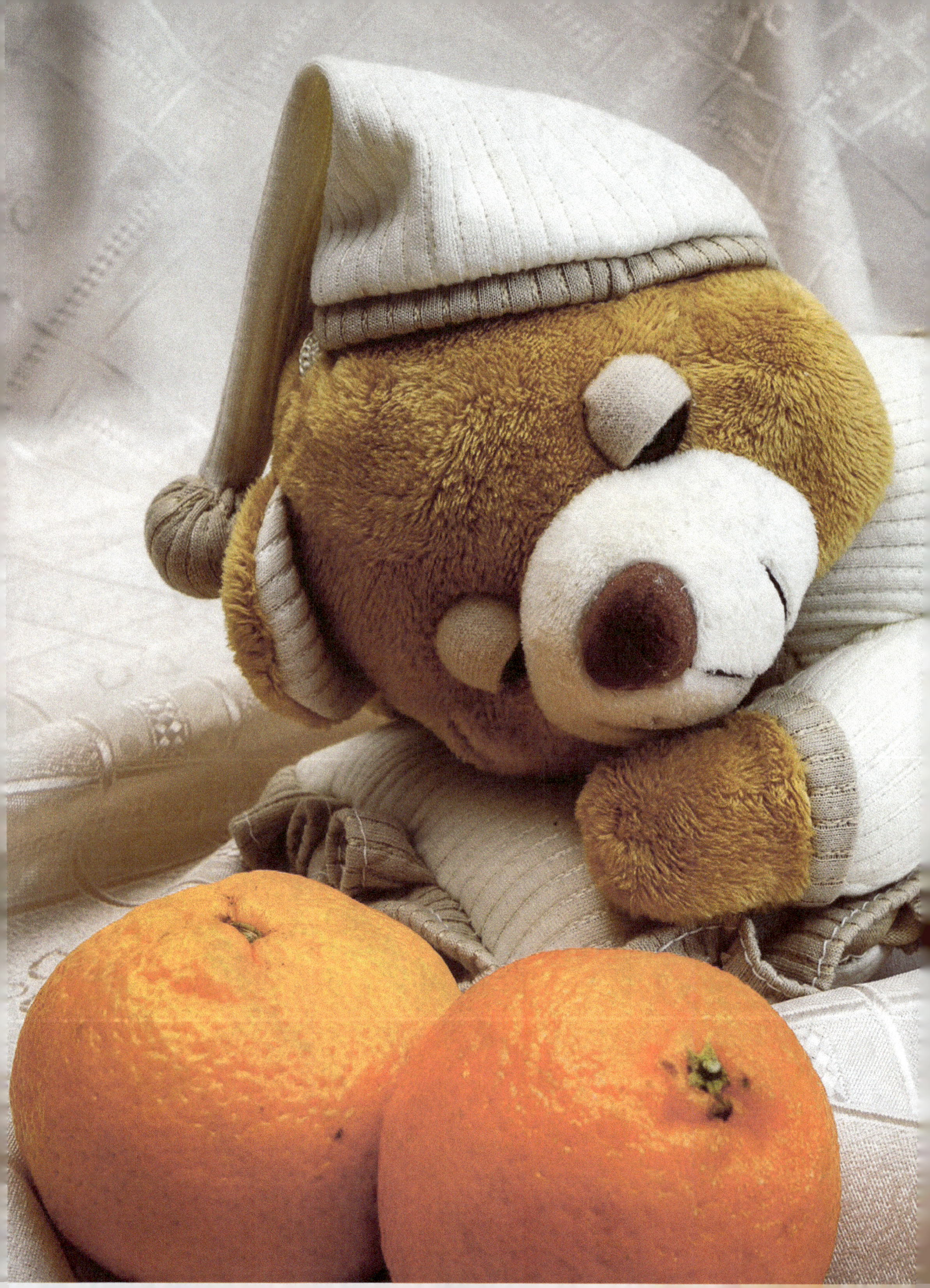

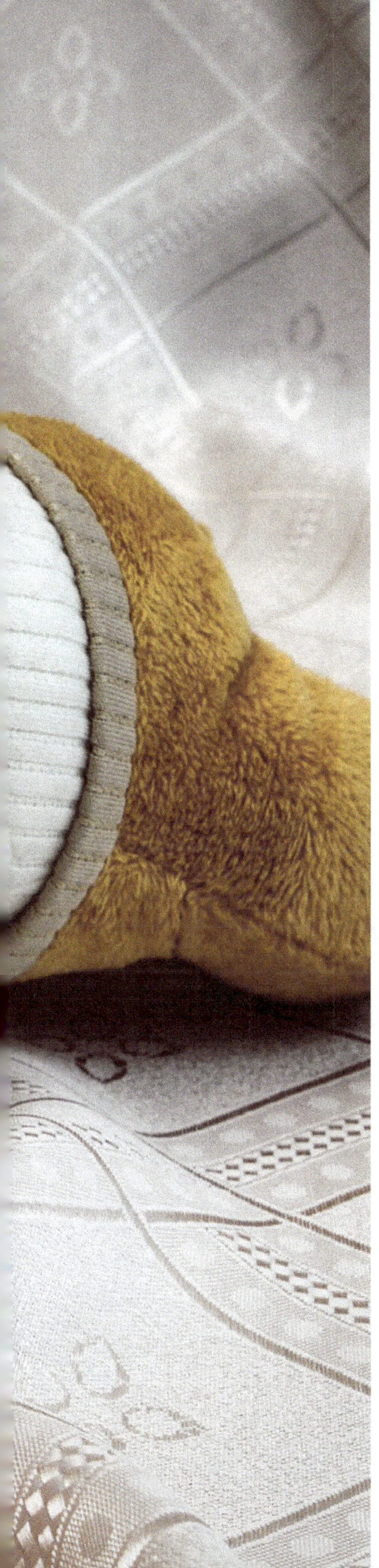

SETTING UP THE CRICUT MAKER

Setting up your Cricut machine is more like unwrapping a Christmas present! You have to be careful, but at the same time, you're eager to get started with it.

The machine setup of any Cricut machine won't take you more than an hour, and there are a few tools that come with the Cricut machine to guide your installation.

Here, we will be using the Cricut Maker to explain the machine setup seeing as it is the newest Cricut technology available.

TOOLS NEEDED

-Cricut Maker.
-Power cord and USB cable.
-Fine point pen.
-A fair point blade.
-Rotatory blade with housing.
-LightGrip Mat 12" by 12".
-FabricGrip Mat 12" by 12".

A computer, tablet, or mobile phone is connected to the internet.
All these tools, except the computer or mobile device, come in the box with the Cricut Maker.

OPENING THE BOX

When you purchase a bundle from Cricut, you will receive a few boxes, but the most significant box amongst them will hold the Cricut Maker. To recognize it, you'll see the picture of the Maker on the box.

When opening the Cricut box, the first thing you see is the welcome packet placed on the machine. The welcome package contains a welcome book, a rotary blade with cover, a fine point pen, a USB cable, and a packet with your first project.

When you take the Cricut machine out of the box, the power cord will be underneath along with the cutting mats.

UNWRAPPING

The Cricut machine is wrapped with a layer of cellophane and a protective wrapper. Before setting up the device, you have to remove the wrappings. Some Styrofoam protects the in-housing of the machine, and that has to go too.

Your Cricut Maker will also come with some supplies, and you should unwrap them and check them out. Lucky for you, the fine point blade is already installed in the Cricut Maker, so you don't have to bother with that.

VISIT CRICUT.COM/SETUP

The next step in setting up your machine lies in the

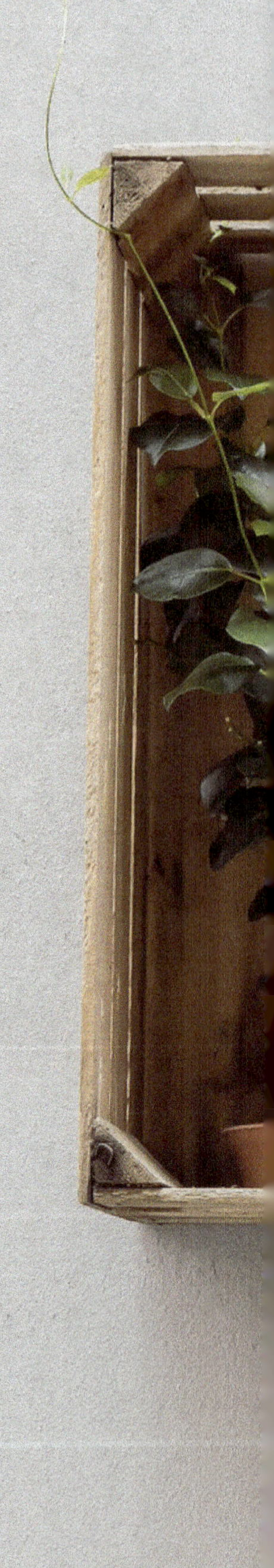

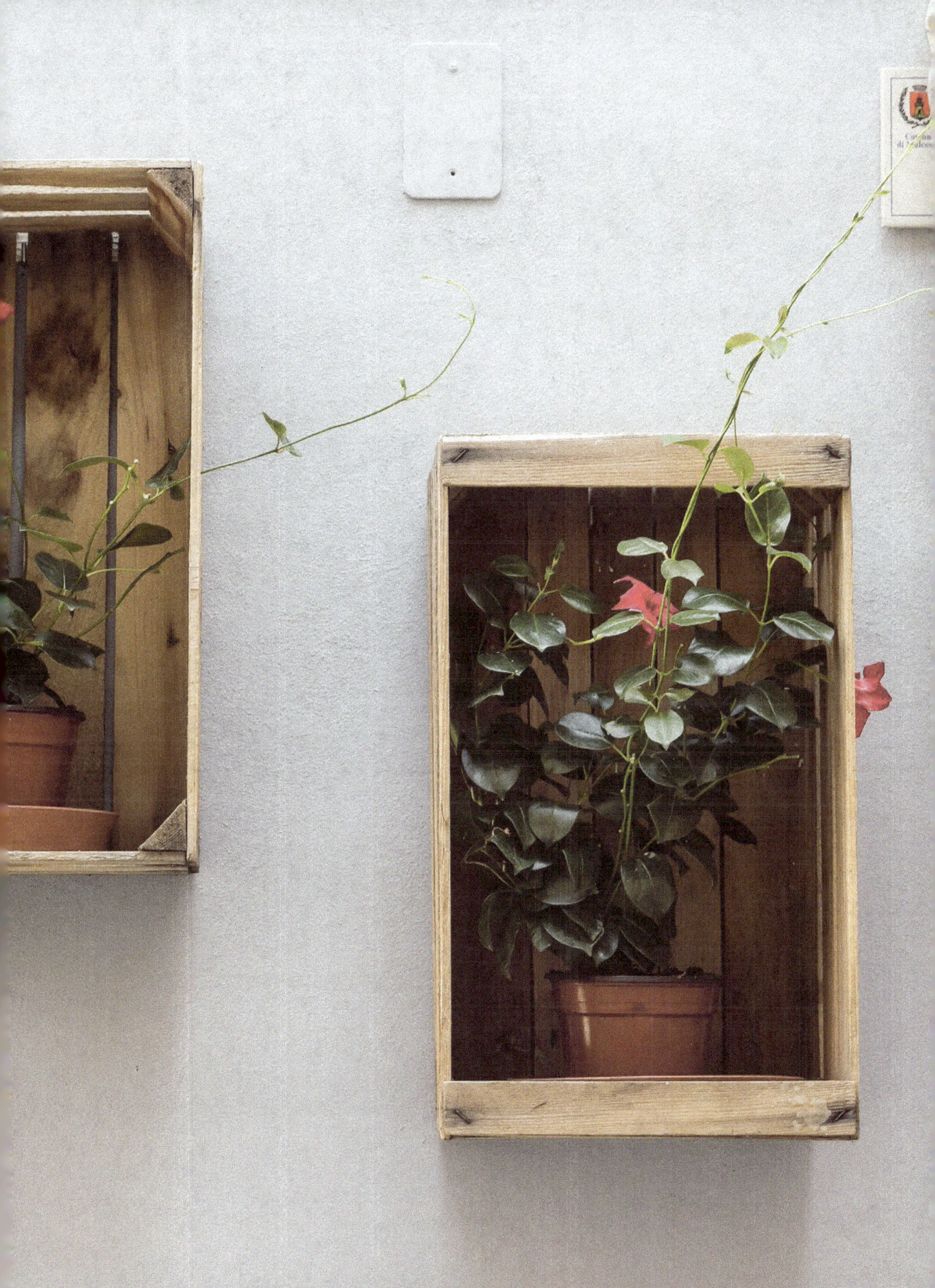

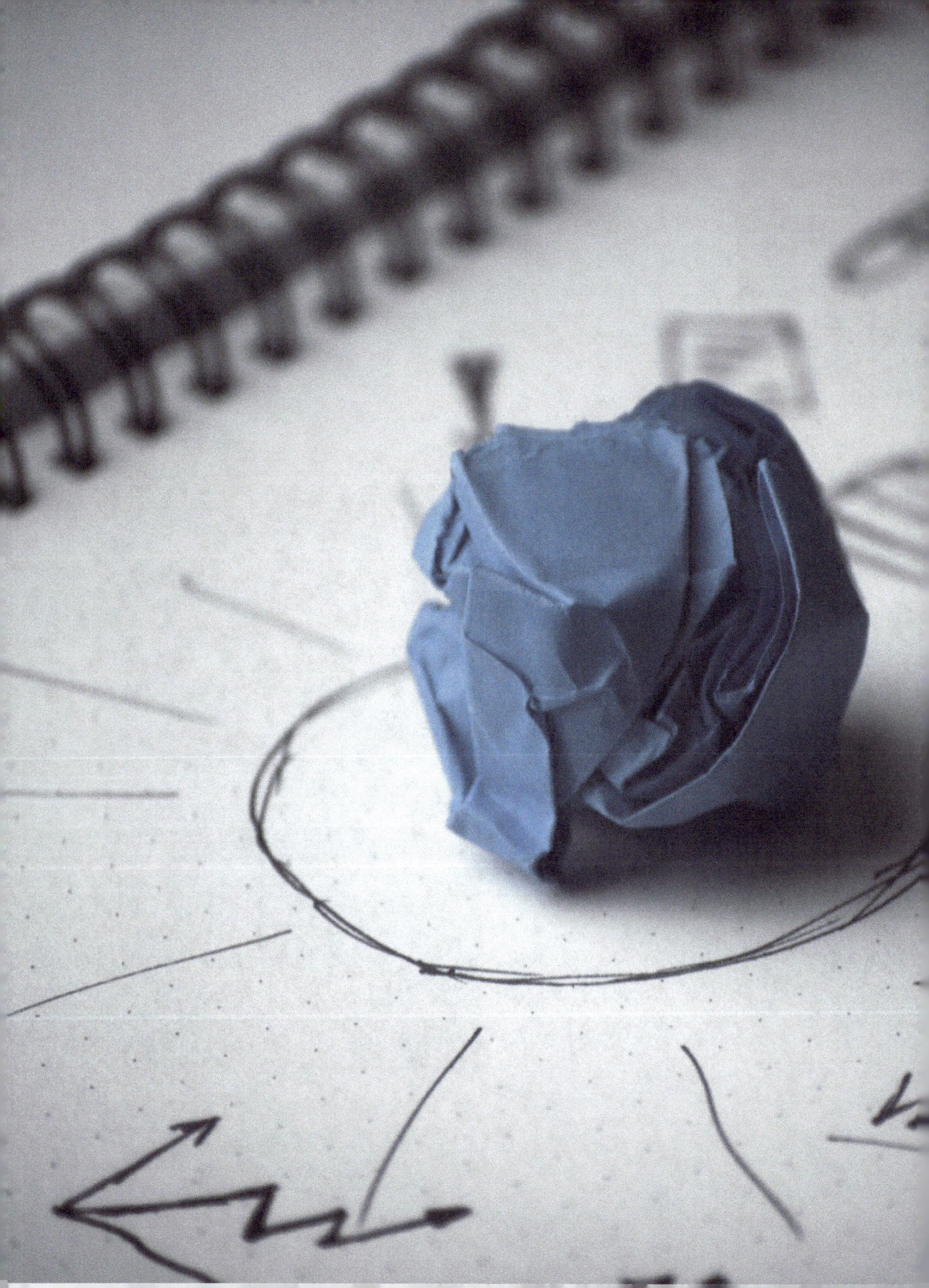

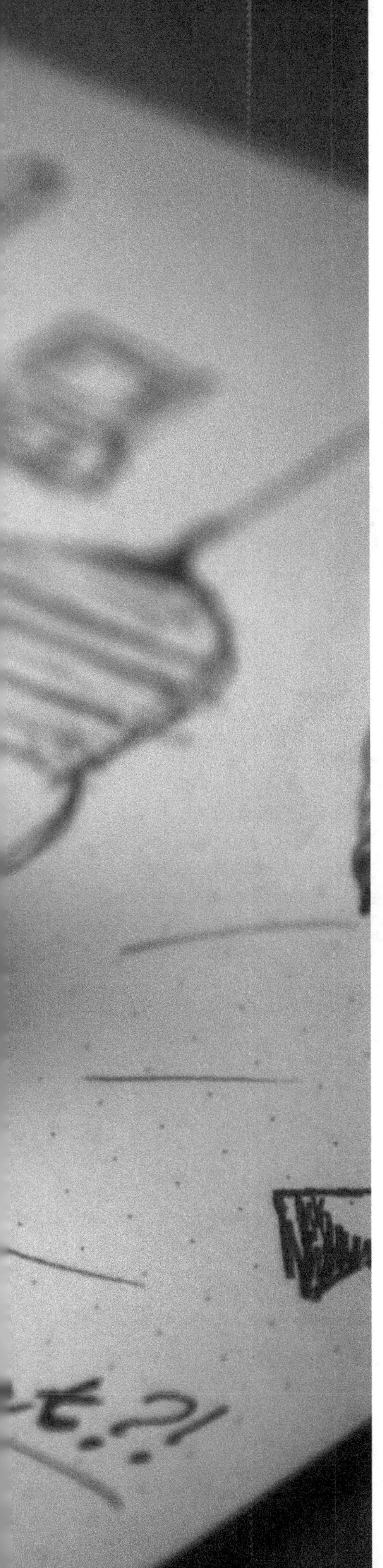

technical aspects. Cricut has a webpage dedicated to walking you through this process, which makes it super easy.

Open cricut.com/setup on your device. You can use any device compatible with Cricut, like a smartphone, tablet, or computer. When you do that, you will be asked to install Cricut Design Space and also sign up. Then, you'll be given your Cricut ID.

If you have been using a former Cricut machine before, you can carry on with your previous ID.

PLUGGING IT IN

Next, you need to take your USB cord and the power cord to power up your Cricut machine.

This will be shown on the setup wizard of the webpage.

For the USB cord, you connect the square end to the Cricut Maker device and the other end to the computer. And, the power cord is easy to connect the Cricut Maker to the power outlet.

CLAIM YOUR BONUS

After plugging in your Cricut, you will be able to claim a free welcome bonus from Cricut, which is a free month of Cricut Access. This means that you get to enjoy access to projects, fonts, and Cricut Cut Files.

BEGIN YOUR PROJECT

If you need a little something to practice before starting your intended project, Cricut Maker machines usually come with a bit of project in the welco-

me pack to help you get acquainted with the tools. The Maker comes with all the tools you need to complete the project, usually making a little card. After this, then you can begin using it. The thing is, when you want to use your Cricut Maker, you need to learn how to use Cricut Design Space.

Chapter 3

How to Use Cricut Maker

After setting up your Cricut maker machine according to the instruction in the previous chapter, there will be directions on your screen that you must follow to create your first project. You will still be using the link you found on the paper when setting up your machine. If you have not yet received your device and are interested in knowing how it works, or you are looking for extra clarifications, here's what it will say.

FIRST STEP

First off, load a pen into the accessories clamp. You can pick whichever color you think will go best with the paper you have received. Next, you want to turn the knob so that the indicator is pointed to "cardstock," considering what you will be working with. Have you had a good look at your mats yet? The blue rug is what you will want to use for this project. You should remove the plastic cover - keep it, don't throw it away as you will need to recover your mat when you're done to avoid dust accumulation - and lay down the paper on the mat with the top left corners of the material and the grid aligned.

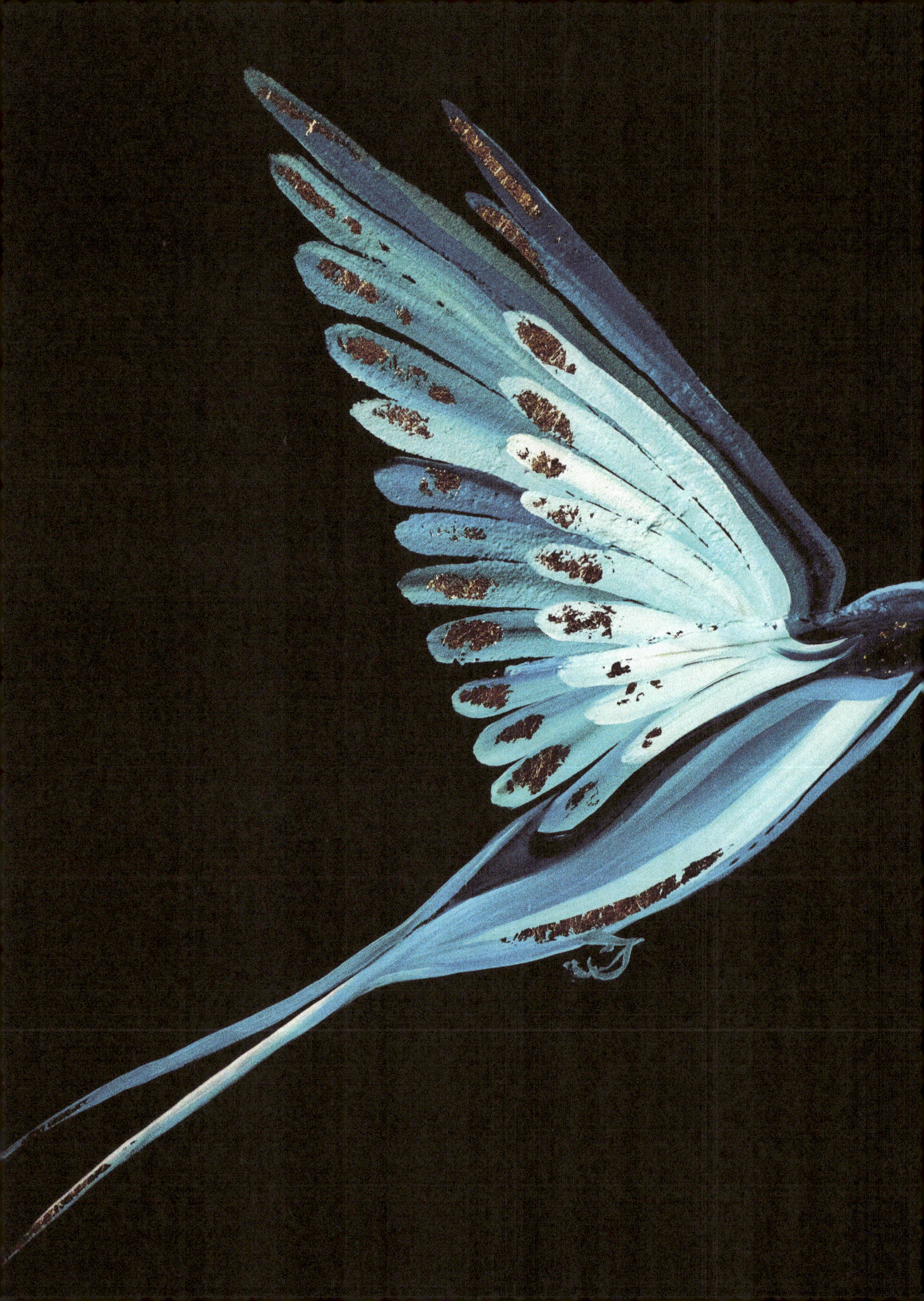

SECOND STEP

Make sure that the paper is pressed flat before you push it between the rollers firmly. The mat has to rest on the bottom roller. When it is in place, press the "Load" button to load your mat between the rollers. Then, all you have to do is press the "go" button, which will be flashing at this stage, and wait for the machine to work its magic on your project. It's cool to watch this process unfold. Once everything is done, the light will flash, and you can press the "Load" button again to unload the mat. Your paper will still be sticking to the mat when you remove it.

THIRD STEP

Be careful when removing the material from the mat. Don't be too hasty; take your time so that it doesn't tear. Pull the meat away from the cardstock instead of doing it the other way around. After completing that step, you can now fold the cardstock in half, insert the liners into the card's corner slots, and it's done!

YOU'RE DONE

You have just made your first ever Cricut project in a matter of minutes from start to finish! Congratulations! You are on your way to becoming a Cricut Master. What are you waiting for? Do more projects! There are a ton of templates you can play around with-practice, practice, practice.

WHAT IS THE DESIGN SPACE?

Design Space is the free design software that comes with each of the Cricut machines. It is very user-friendly and, as such, is easy to use. It is a cloud-based software solution that means that all project files are accessible on any device from anywhere you have Internet access.
Design Space is compatible with Windows, MAC, iOS, and Android, giving a wide range of device options to work on. Most of the newer Cricut machines also have Bluetooth options, making it easy to connect with mobile devices.

IINSTALL THE DESIGN SPACE TO YOUR COMPUTER

To download the Design Space plugin and install, it is super simple. To know that your setup process is complete is when you are prompted to start your first project.

FOR IOS/ANDROID

Use the power outlet to plug your Cricut machine.
Power ON your Cricut machine
Pair your Cricut machine with your iOS or Android device via Bluetooth

Download the Design Space plugin and install it.

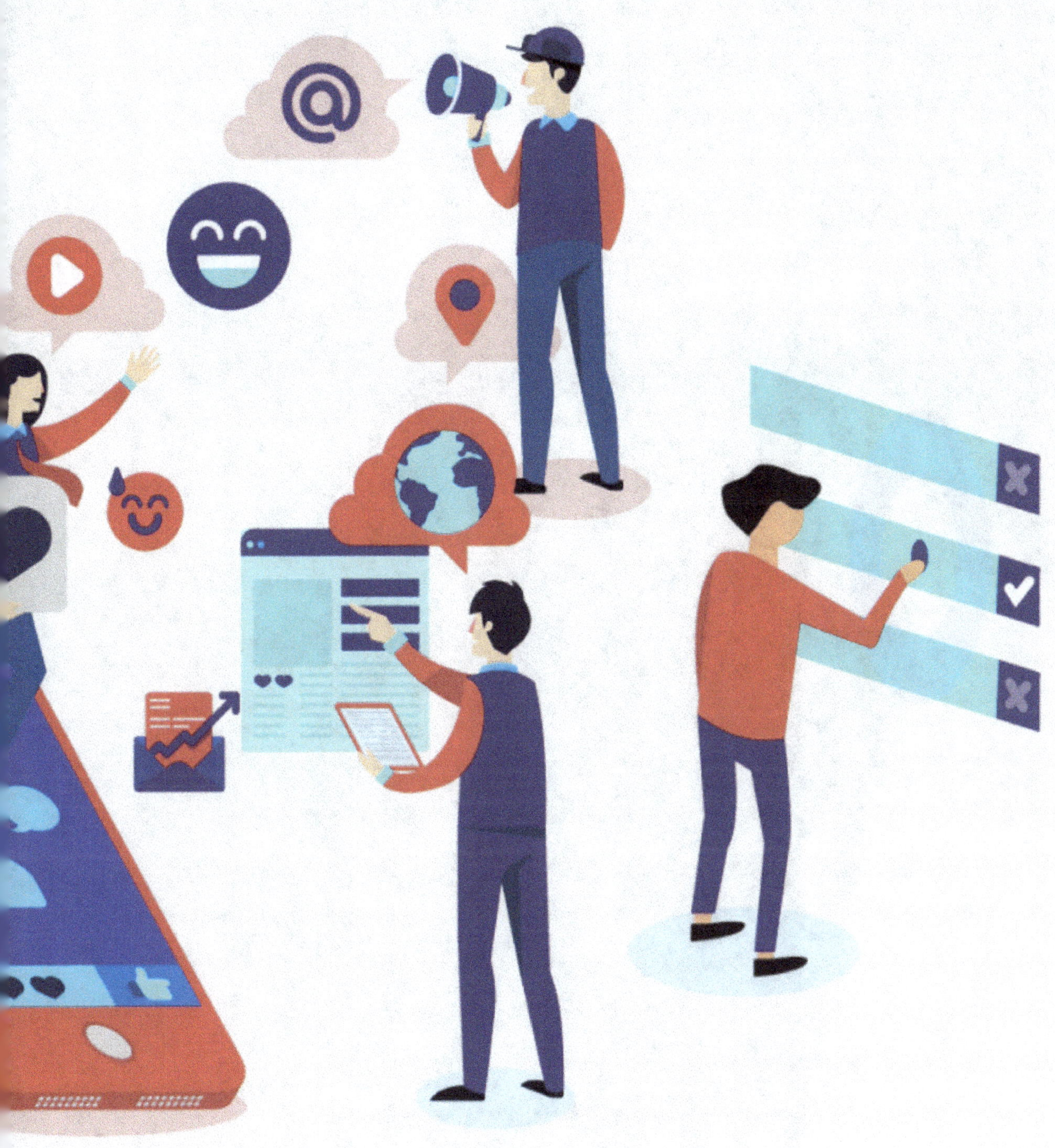

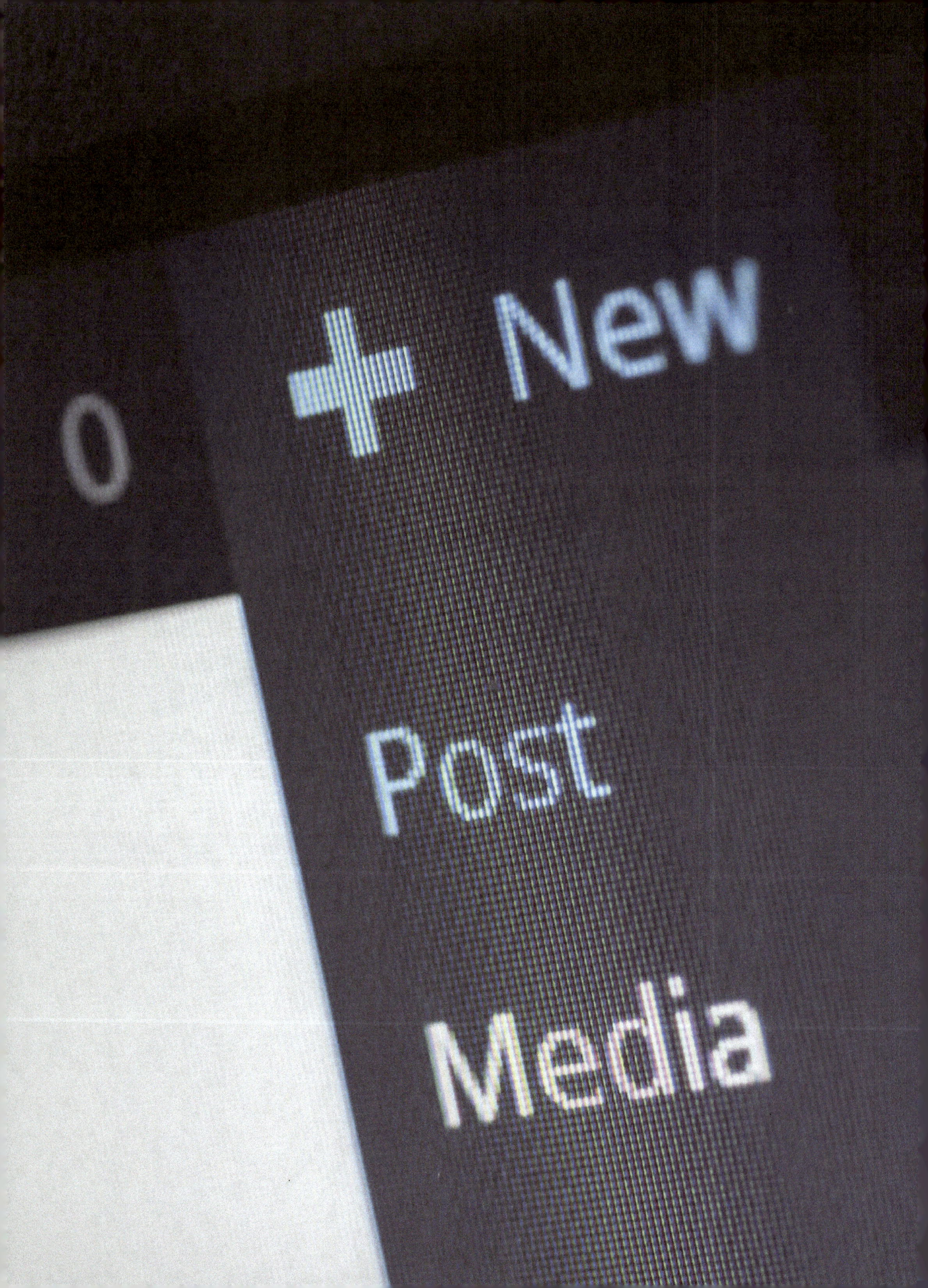

0
+ New
Post
Media

Launch the downloaded app

Create a Cricut ID to sign in and if you have one already, use it to sign in

Select the menu and tap Machine Setup & App Overview

Tap New Machine Setup

Follow the prompts on your screen to finish the setup
Again, to know that your setup process is complete is when you are prompted to start your first project. Note that your machine is registered automatically during the setup process of your Cricut machine. There is no cause for alarm if, for any reason, you did not complete the process when you first connect your computer to your Cricut machine. Go to step 5 and continue from there using the onscreen instructions.

WORKSPACE/CANVAS

The workspace is where you will position images, shapes, text, etc., to create your projects. Cricut refers to the workspace as the canvas, as it is where you will make your works of art. It is the largest part of the workspace and is in the middle of the screen.
The canvas consists of a grid representing inches as the default setting and runs across from 0 to 60, the x-axis. The y-axis runs from 0 down to 60. The workspace has a ruler along the top and down the left-hand side of it.

Although you can do big projects and lay them out on the screen, the Cricut machines generally use 12" x 12" cutting mats. This means that any more significant projects than 12" x 12" will need to be cut in stages.

ZOOM CONTROL

Located on the bottom of the canvas, you will find the zoom control. It is not visible until you roll the mouse over it.
This is a convenient tool for larger projects as it allows you to zoom into the project to see the bigger picture.

DESIGN PANEL

The design panel is located to the left of the canvas. It is where you can reset or create new projects, select templates, images, shapes, text, or upload your ideas.
The design panel consists of the following menu options (from top to bottom):

NEW

The 'New' menu option refreshes the canvas to start a new project. It is like putting a brand-new canvas on an easel to create a new painting.

TEMPLATES

The 'Template' option will place an outline on the screen of various items to better visualize the

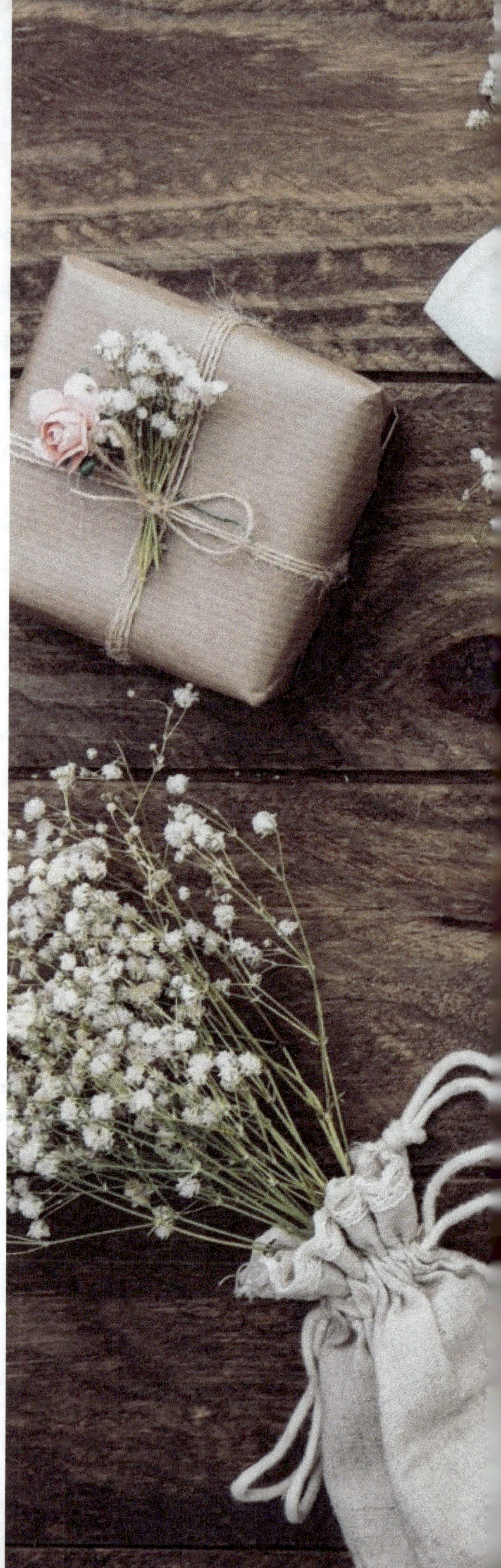

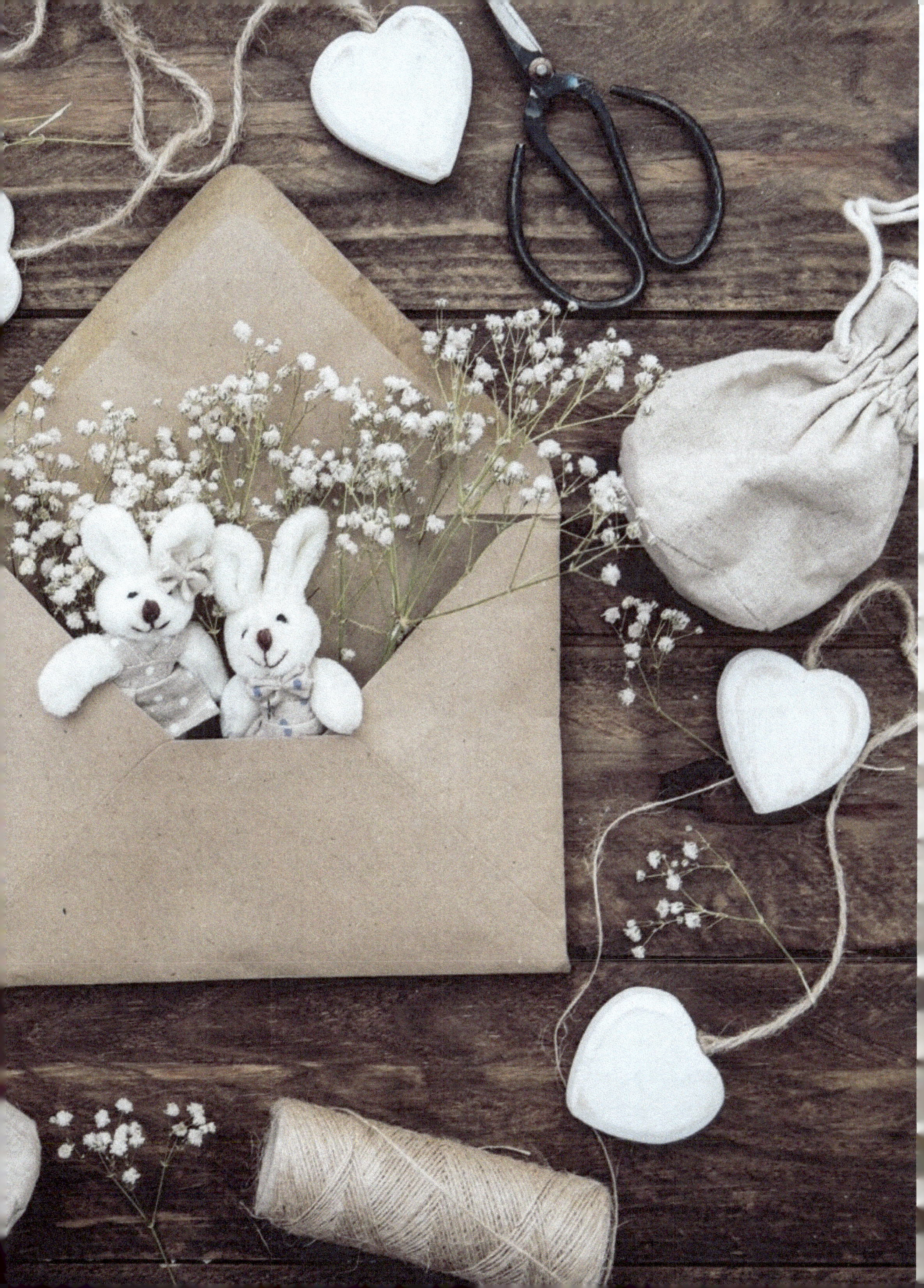

project. For instance, if you were going to design T-Shirt logos, you would choose the 'Template' option and search for a T-Shirt. A template offering the front and back views of a T-Shirt will show on the canvas. You can customize some of these templates' sizes and shapes, depending on the template's characteristics. It is good to note, however, that templates do not cut or print out. They are only for display purposes.

PROJECTS

Cricut has libraries full of ready-to-create projects that you can buy to help you get started. The wonderful thing about these projects is that you can customize them. For Cricut beginners, they are a great way to learn about using various shapes and designs.

IMAGES

Cricut comes loaded with libraries of various images. There are both free images and those that you have to buy. But the price is minimal, and if you do not have the time to create your own, they can be instrumental. You can also buy cartridges that contain different image libraries.

TEXT

To put text on the screen, choose the 'Text' option. Cricut comes with system fonts, fonts that can be purchased, and some free Cricut

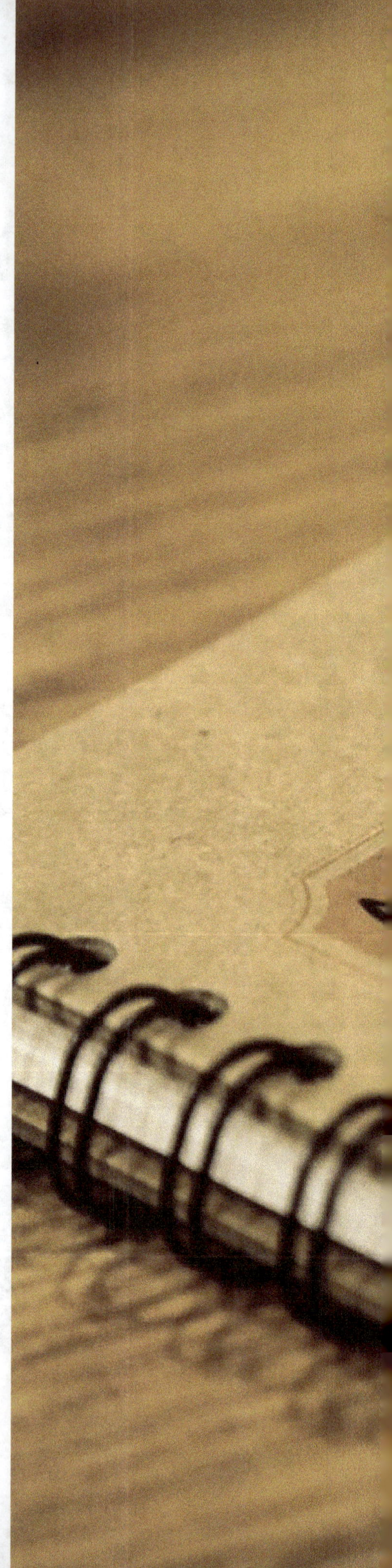

CAFÉ USA
MCDONALD'S
CÀNG UỐNG CÀNG PHÊ
SÀI GÒN
HAI LỚP BÒ
BÁNH MÌ MEI
BIC MAC
IN THE WORLD
TÔI YÊU SÀI GÒN
SÀI GÒN CÀNG VUI
SỮA ĐÁ
SINCE 2014

fonts.

SHAPES

The 'Shapes' option allows you to use shapes on the canvas. There are quite a few standard shapes offered that you could learn to manipulate to create additional ones as you get more familiar with Cricut. The score lines are used to hold marks for folding projects such as cards or gift boxes. They mark the fold lines.

UPLOAD

Upload is where you can upload your projects, designs, and images, or projects that you may have purchased or downloaded from the various websites that offer already-made projects.

HEADER BAR

The header bar is the dark grey bar at the top of the canvas. This bar holds the following options and information:

THREE HORIZONTAL BARS

When clicked, the three bars drop down into a menu of options. These options are for setting up the machine, changing basic software settings, legal notices, managing custom materials, and so on.

CANVAS

The Canvas option helps you navigate back to the current canvas from the Home Screen, images, templates, etc.

PAGE TITLE

The page title will start as 'Untitled' for new projects until they are saved. If you open a saved project, the name of that project is reflected.

MY PROJECTS

The 'My Projects' option is a shortcut to open up previously saved projects.

SAVE

The 'Save' option is a shortcut to use when you want to save your project. You should keep your projects every few minutes or when you have completed a section of a project.

MAKE IT

The 'Make It's green button is the 'Go' button to send your project to the pre-cut phase. Here, you can check the boards and the way that the project is going to be cut. You will send the project to the inkjet for print and cut. This is where you will set up custom materials and blade selection, depth, etc., for the machine.

EDIT BAR

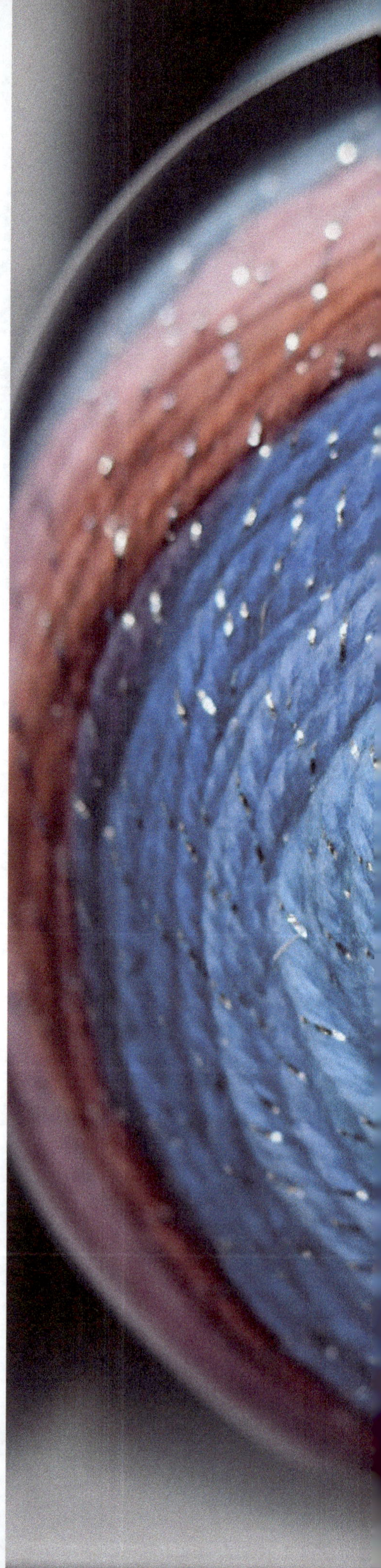

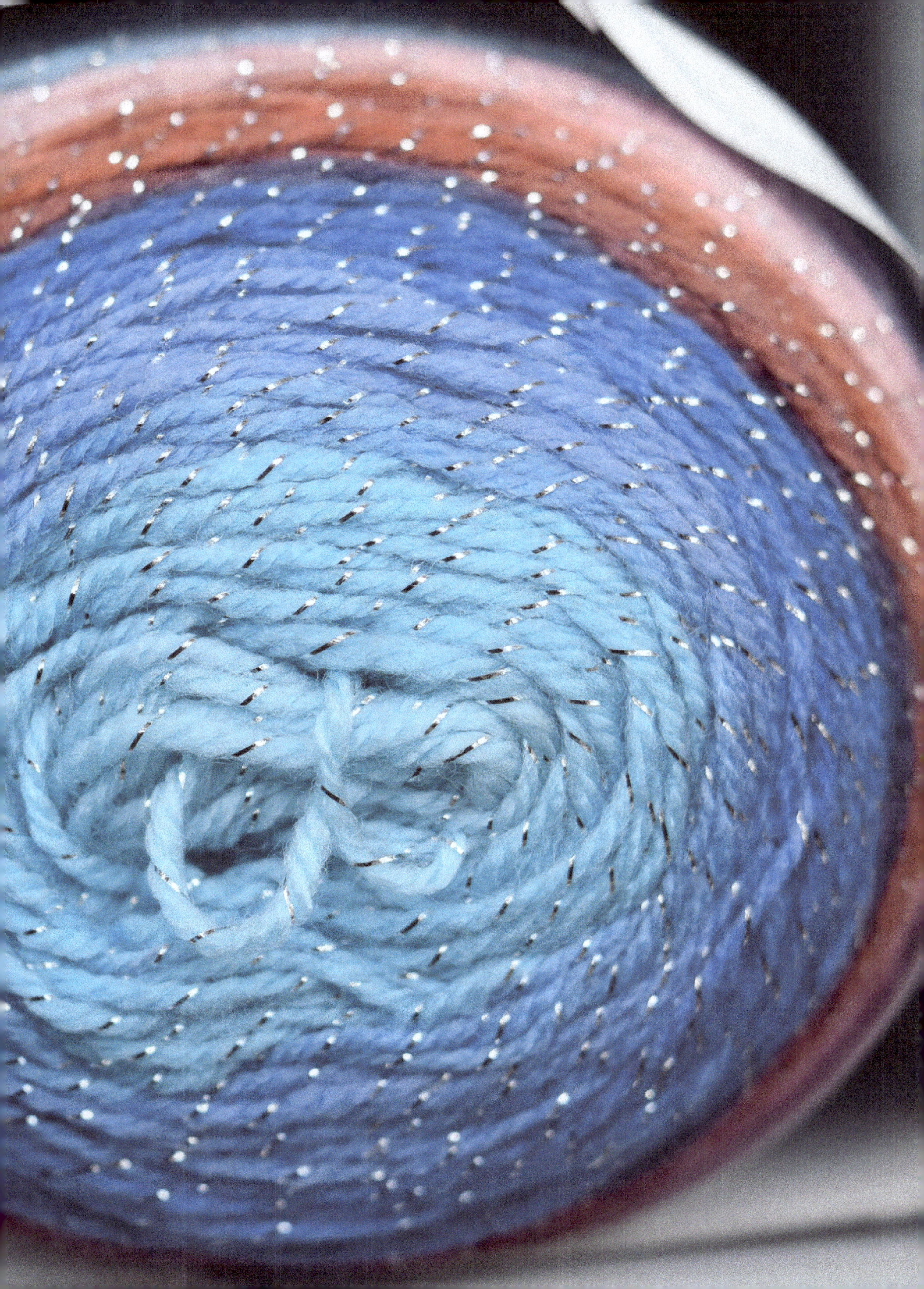

The edit bar remains grayed out until an image, shape, template, or text is placed on the canvas. It is located directly beneath the header bar but now on top of the canvas.

The selected object on the canvas determines the options on the edit bar:

TEMPLATES

When you use a template, the edit bar will tell you if you can adjust the template. The system predetermines these; you will need to select based on what the template has been designed with. The edit bar will list the changes you can make; for instance, a T-Shirt template gives the option of 'Type,' 'Size,' and 'Color.'

COMMON OPTIONS

There are some standard options that both text and images used on the edit bar. These are options are:

UNDO

This will undo the latest edit, addition, or deletion.

REDO

This will redo something that has recently been undone.

LINETYPE

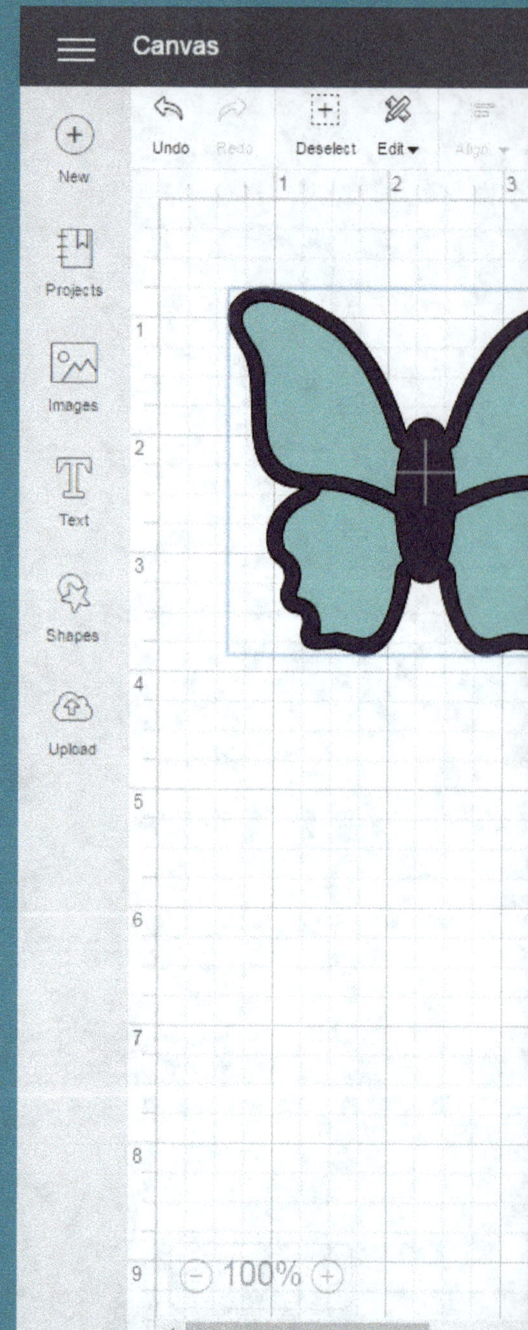

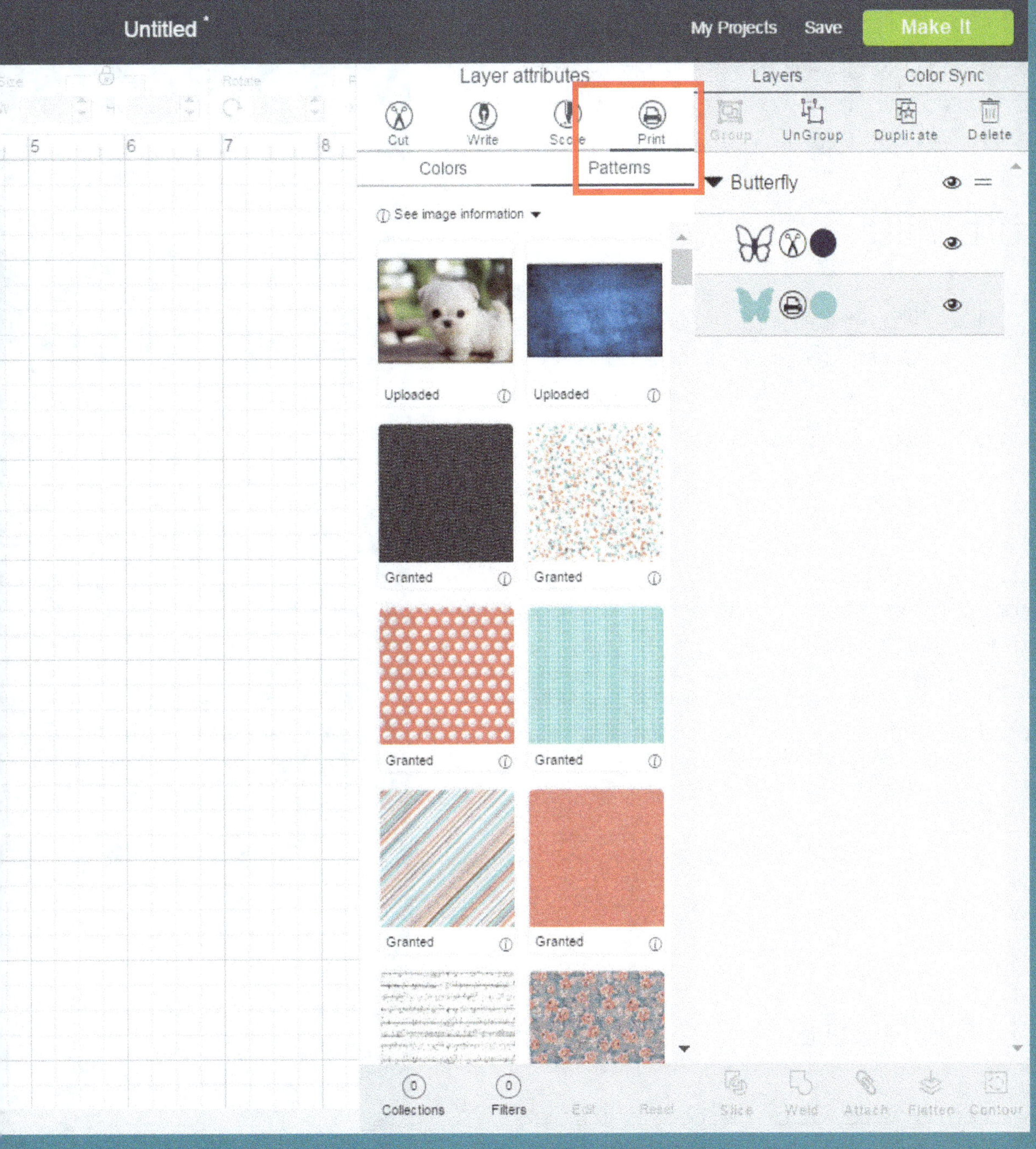

This option tells the Cricut to use a blade to 'Cut,' 'Draw' with a pen, or use the Scoring stylus or wheel to create a scoreline. You can 'Deboss' with the debossing tip, 'Engrave' with the engraving tool, and change a line to perforated, which is 'Perf' or wavy 'Wave.' These are add-on tools to use with the Cricut
.

LINETYPE SWATCH

This is the little box next to the 'Linetype.' When you click on the box, it will bring up a color swatch. This will change the color of the object selected on the screen.

FILL

The 'Fill' option is used for cutting or printing. This option tells Design Space where to send the project to first. It is used for print and cut projects.

FILL SWATCH

This will change the fill of the object selected on the screen.

SELECT ALL/DESELECT

This is used to select all of the objects on the screen at once. When used, the option will change to 'Deselect.'

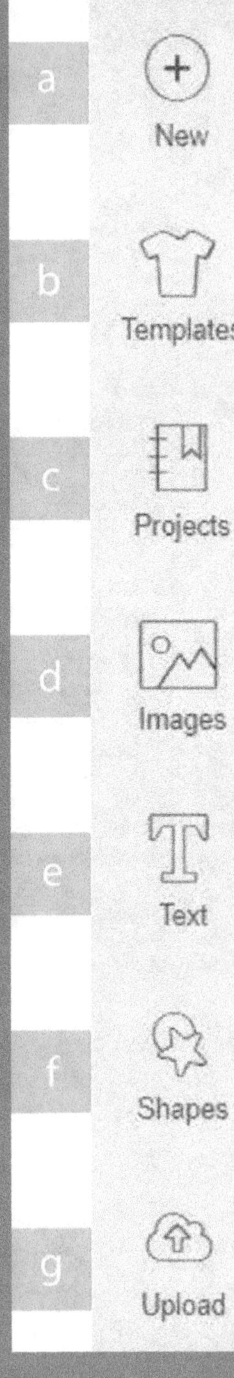

a
New
b
Templates
c
Projects
d
Images
e
Text
f
Shapes
g
Upload

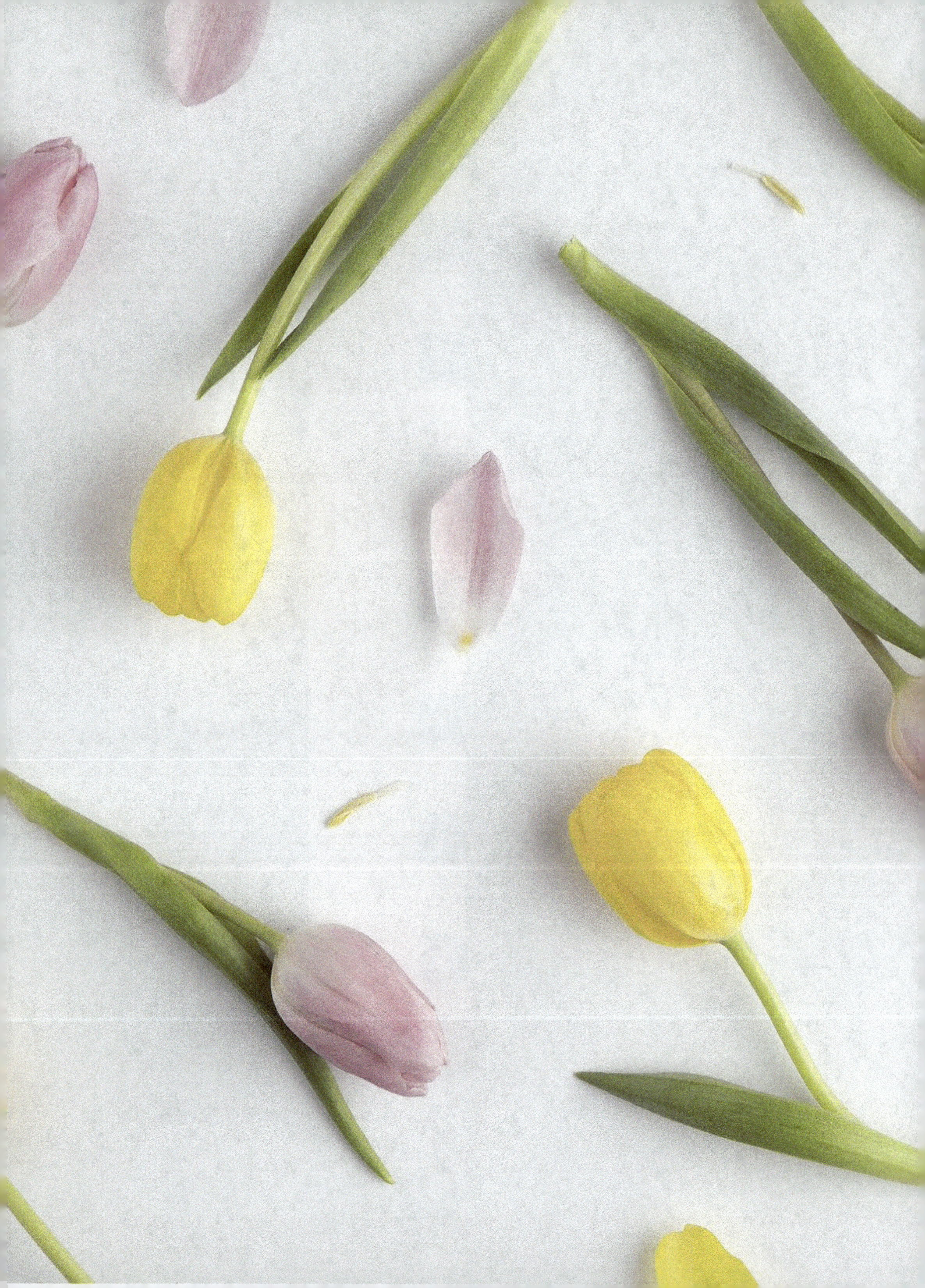

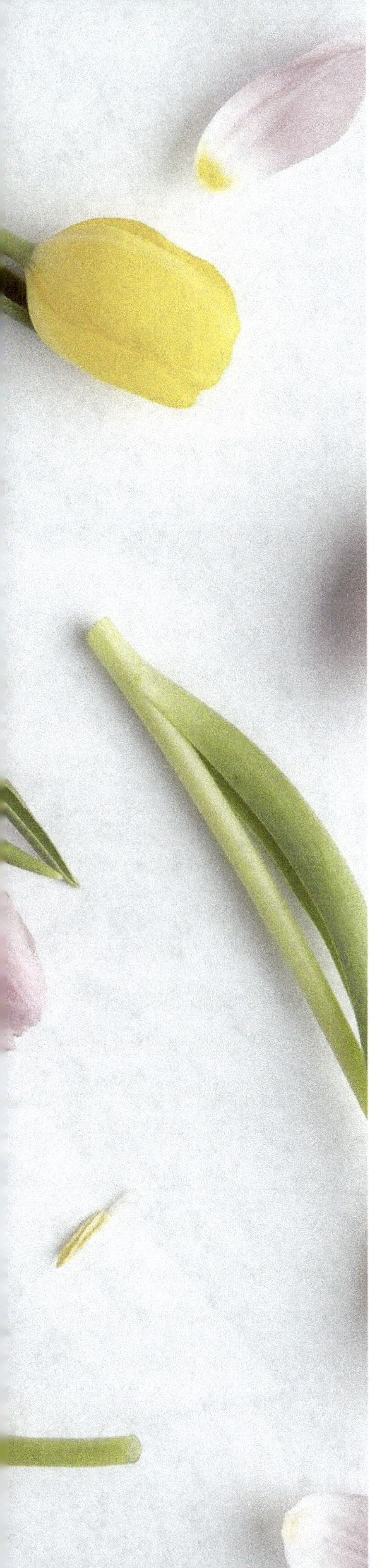

EDIT

The 'Edit' option is where you will find the editing options such as 'Cut,' 'Copy,' and 'Paste.'

ALIGN

The 'Align' function helps align objects with the top, bottom, center, left, right, etc. It can also be used to distribute selected items on the screen evenly.

ARRANGE

The 'Arrange' function changes how objects appear on the screen when they are layered on top of each other. There is a stacking order to objects when they are layered on the screen. 'Send to Back' sends the selected object to the bottom of the layer stack. 'Move Backwards' moves the selected object one layer back. 'Send to Front' sends the selected item to the top of the coating. 'Move Forward' sends the selected object one layer forward.

FLIP

This option is used to flip the image horizontally or vertically to create a shadow image or mirrored image.

SIZE

You can change the selected objects' size on the screen by selecting them and dragging them with the mouse. This option allows you to size the chosen item or entire text box more accurately if you need an exact size. You can set the width and height of an unlocked object. Locked objects will set to scale.

ROTATE

This option rotates the selected object by the degree you set in the box.

POSITION

You can move selected objects around the screen by selecting them and dragging them with the mouse. For more accurate positioning, you can set the x-axis and y-axis positions in these boxes.

FONT

There are different types of fonts to choose from. Some are free, and some can be purchased. The system will also pick up the system fonts you have installed on the device you are working on.

STYLE

This option allows you to change the font's style to Bold, Italic, Underline, Bold, and Underline Regular or Writing.

FONT SIZE

Set the font to the necessary size.

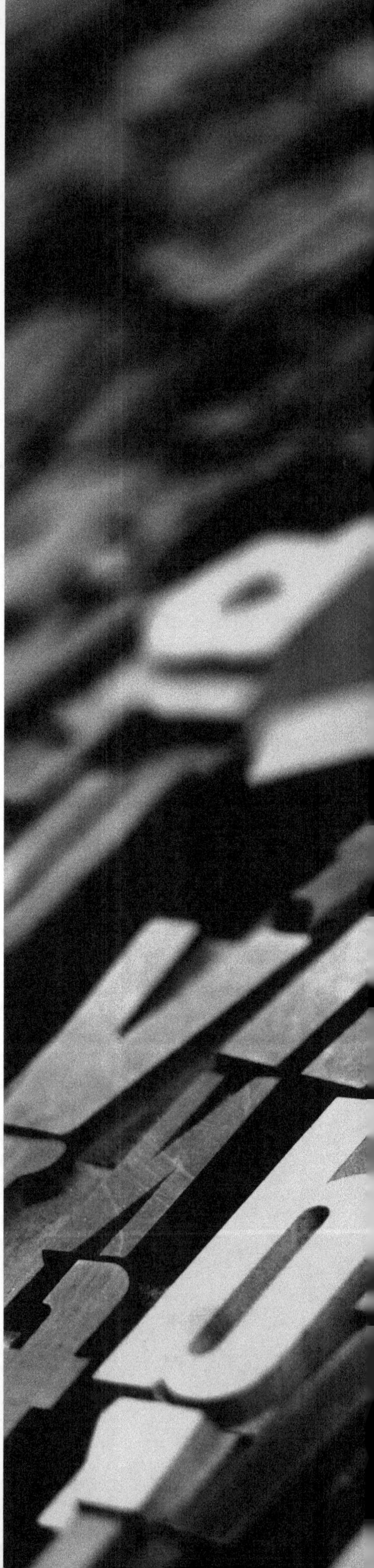

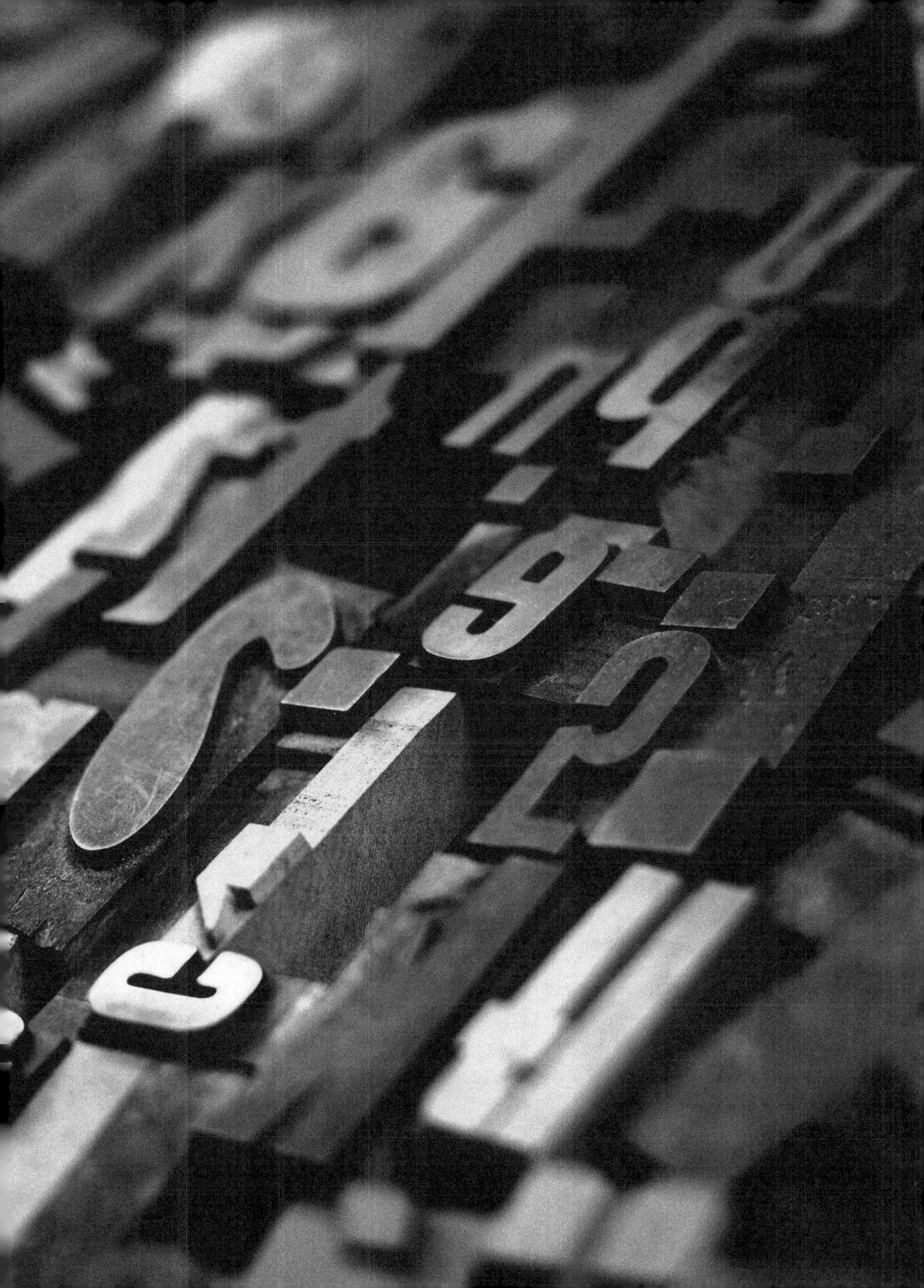

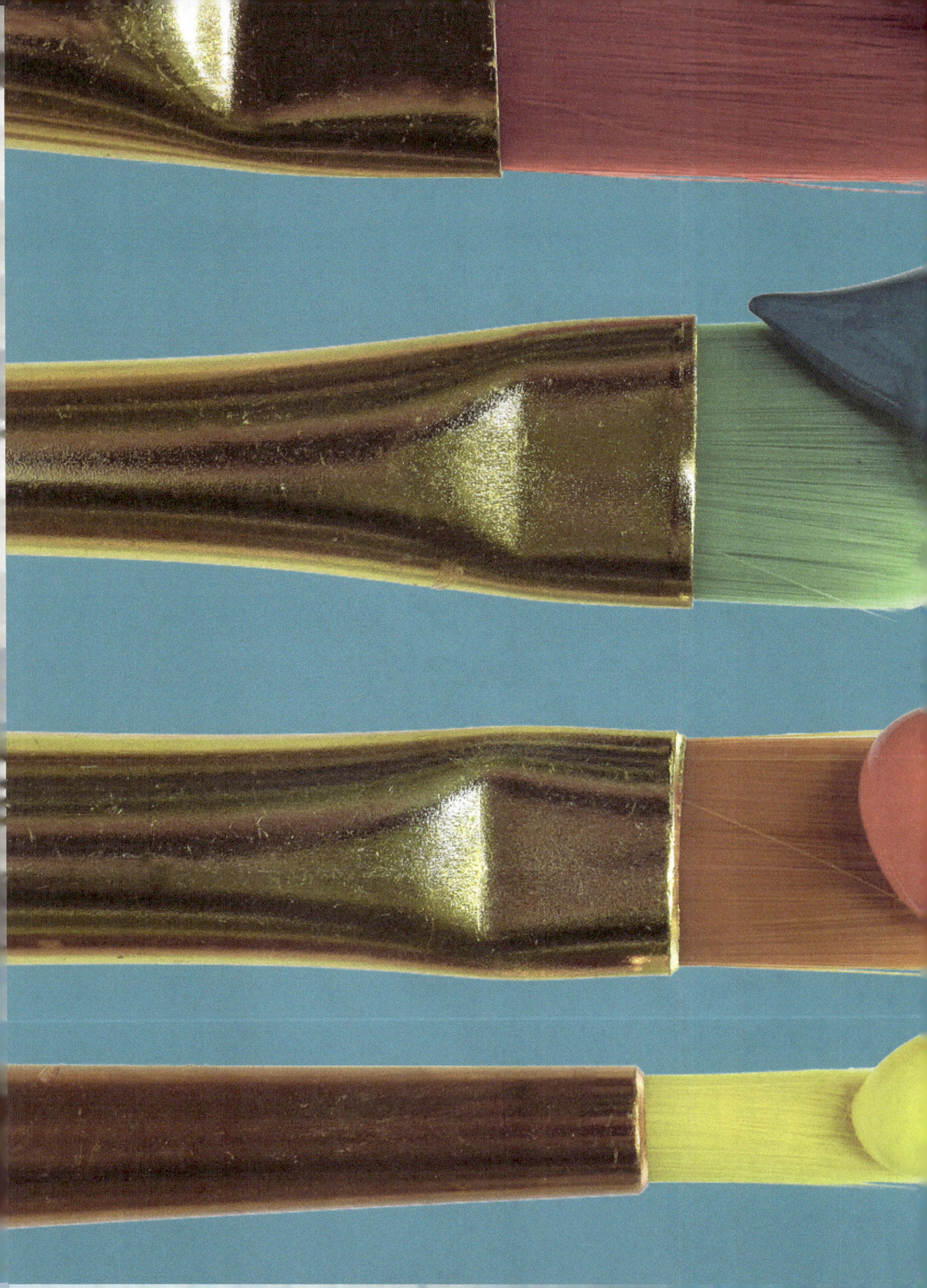

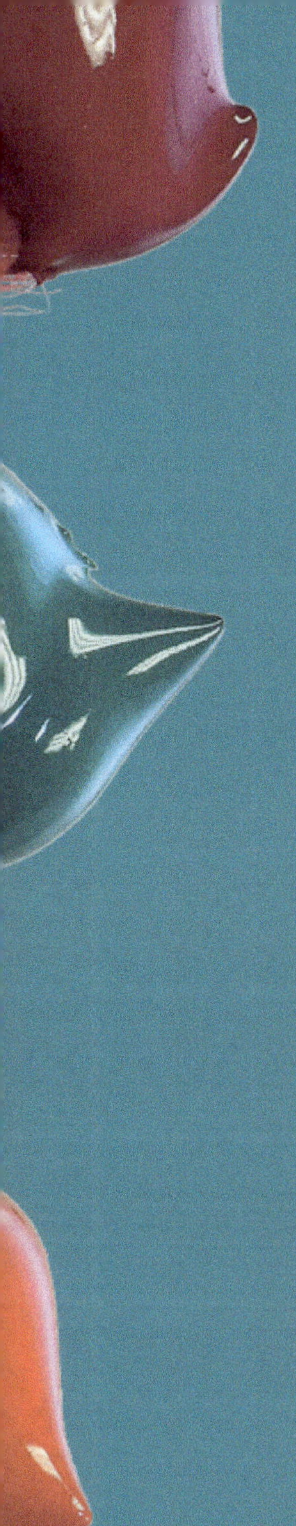

LETTER SPACE

This option is used to increase or decrease the space between letters in a word.

LAYERS PANEL

The layers panel is located to the right of the canvas. This shows the different layers of an object. It has a few useful tools that you will need when you are creating your projects.

COLOR SYNC PANEL

The color sync panel can be found on the right-hand side of the canvas and is the tab next to the layers panel.
This panel is useful when working with multiple colors to cut down on the number of materials the project will call for.

Chapter 4
What Cricut Maker Can Cut

Garment Leather	Tooling Leather	Acetate
Adhesive Foil	Adhesive Sheet	Aluminum Foil
Balsa	Bamboo Fabric	Basswood
Bengaline	Birch	Boucle
Broadcloth	Burlap	Burnt-out Velvet
Calico	Cambric	Canvas
Carbon Fiber	Cardstock	Cashmere
Cereal Box	Chalkboard Vinyl	Challis

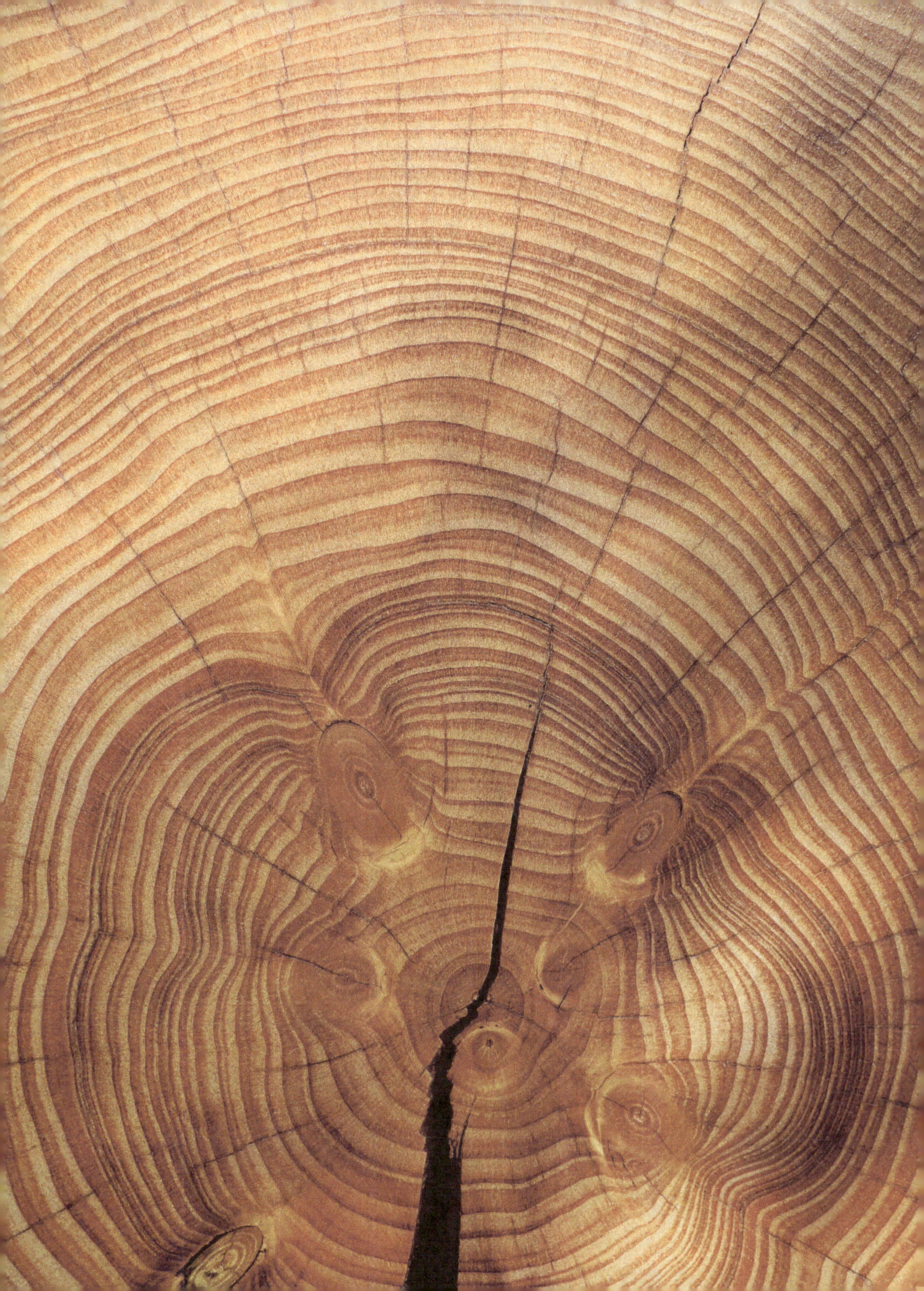

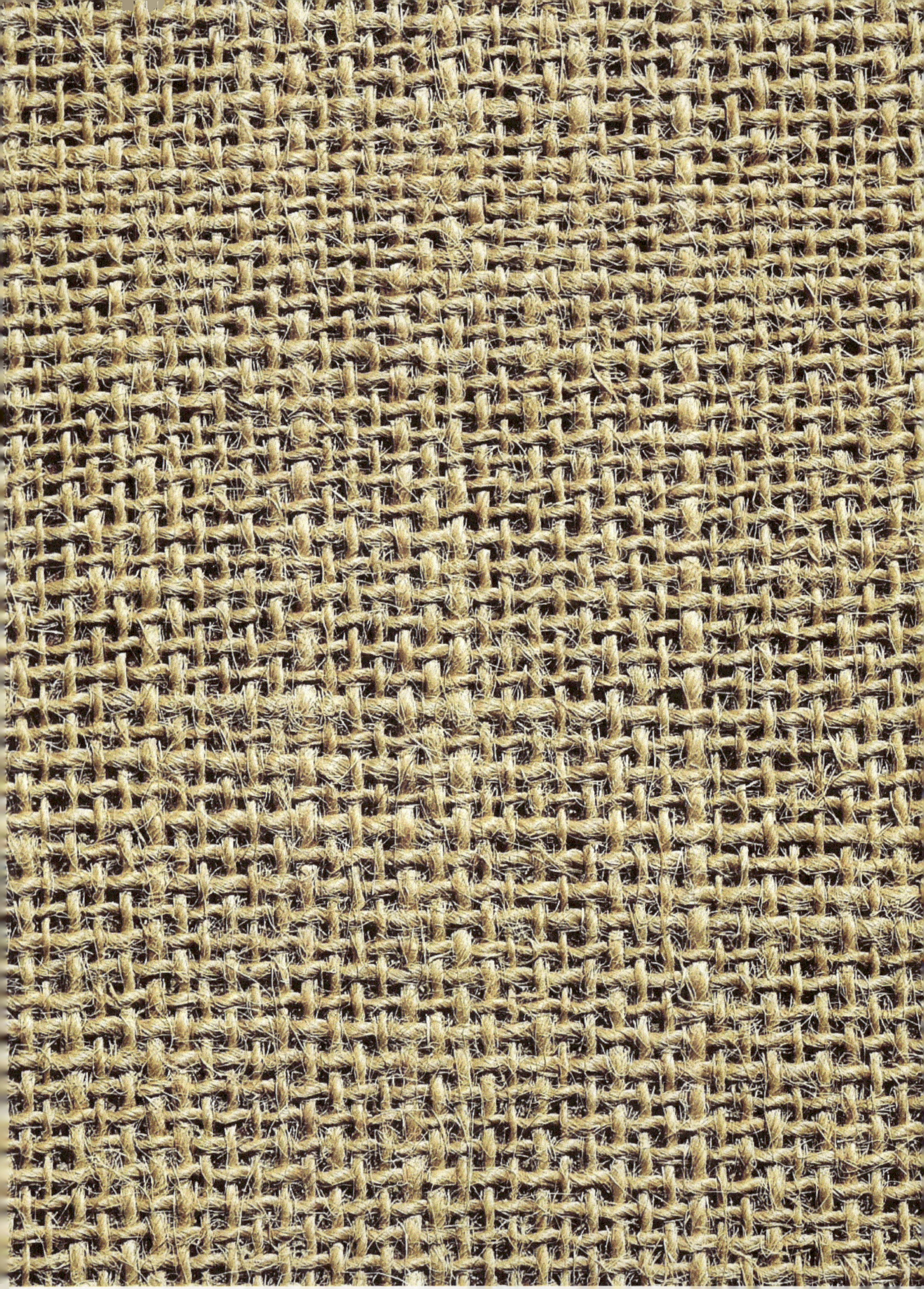

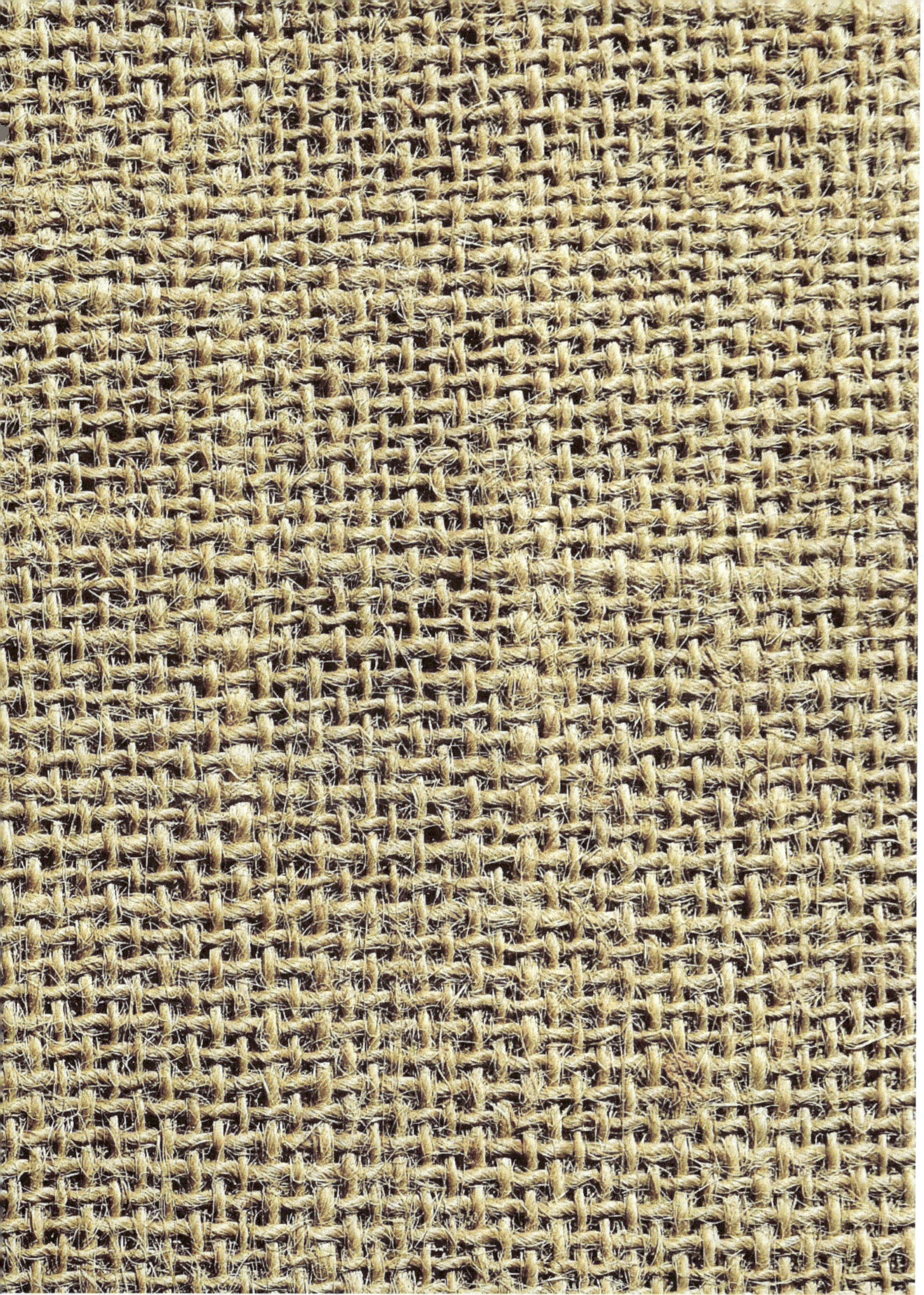

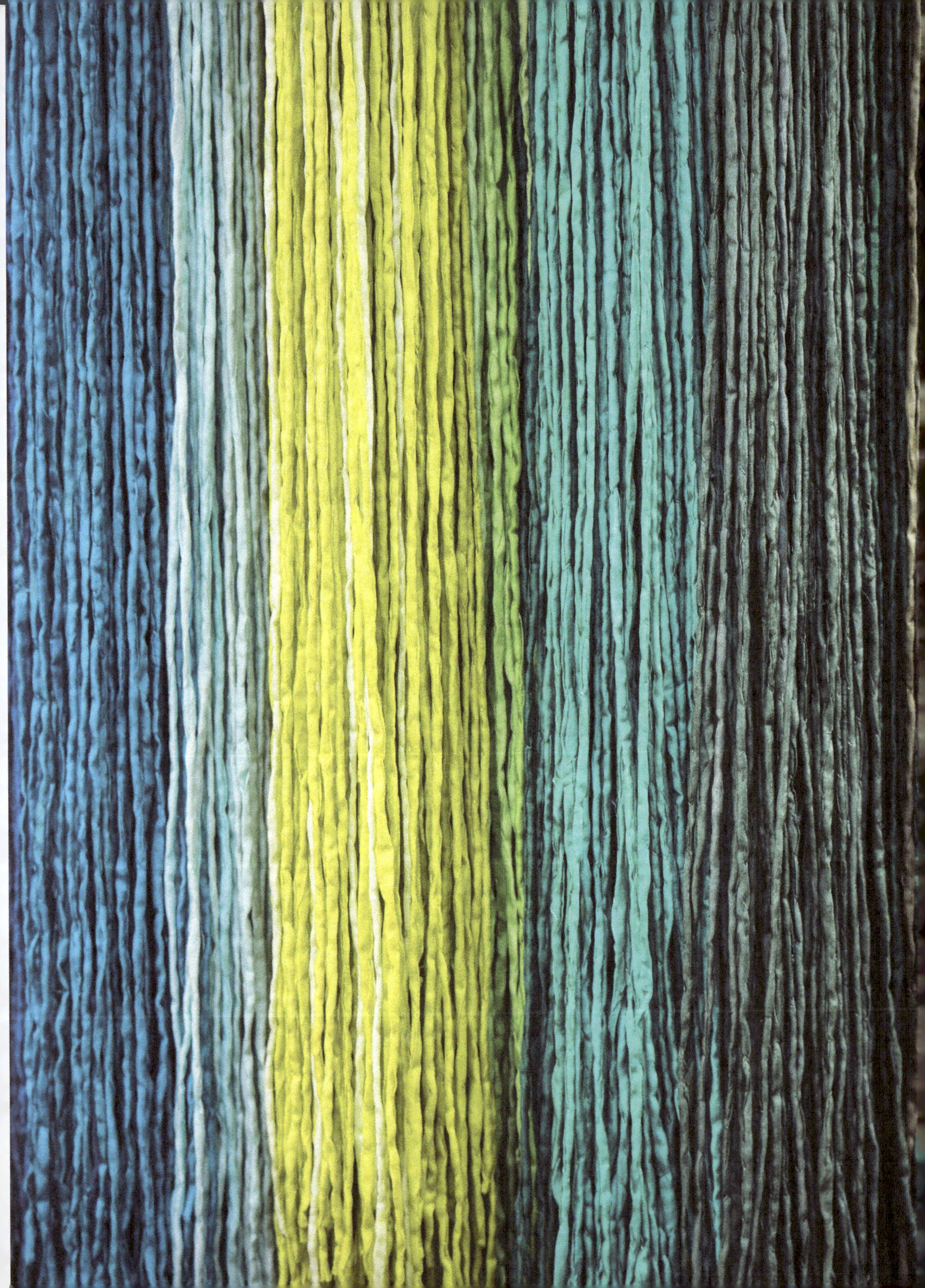

Chambray	Chantilly Lace	Chiffon
Charmeuse Satin	Chintz	Corduroy
Corrugated Paper and Cardboard	Cotton	Crepe Charmeuse
Damask	Tulle	Denim
Duck Cloth	Duct Tape Sheet	Dupion Silk
EVA Foam	Faille	Faux Fur
Felt	Fleece	Freezer Paper
Gabardine	Gauze	Georgette
Gossamer	Grosgrain	Heather
Jacquard	Jersey	Jute
Khaki	Lame	Linen
Lycra	Magnetic Sheet	Matboard
Matelassé	Matte Vinyl	Melton Wool
Mesh	Microfiber	Moleskin

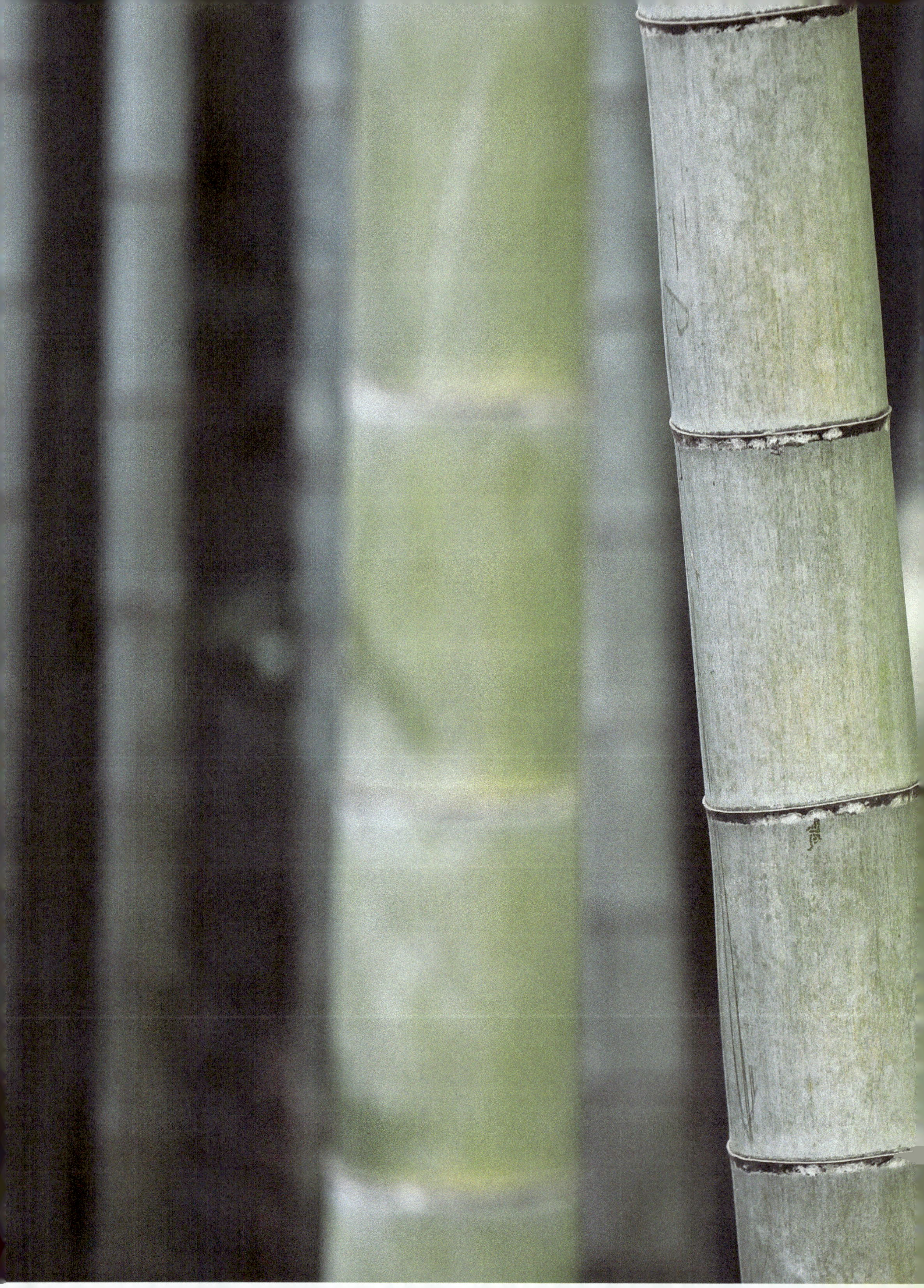

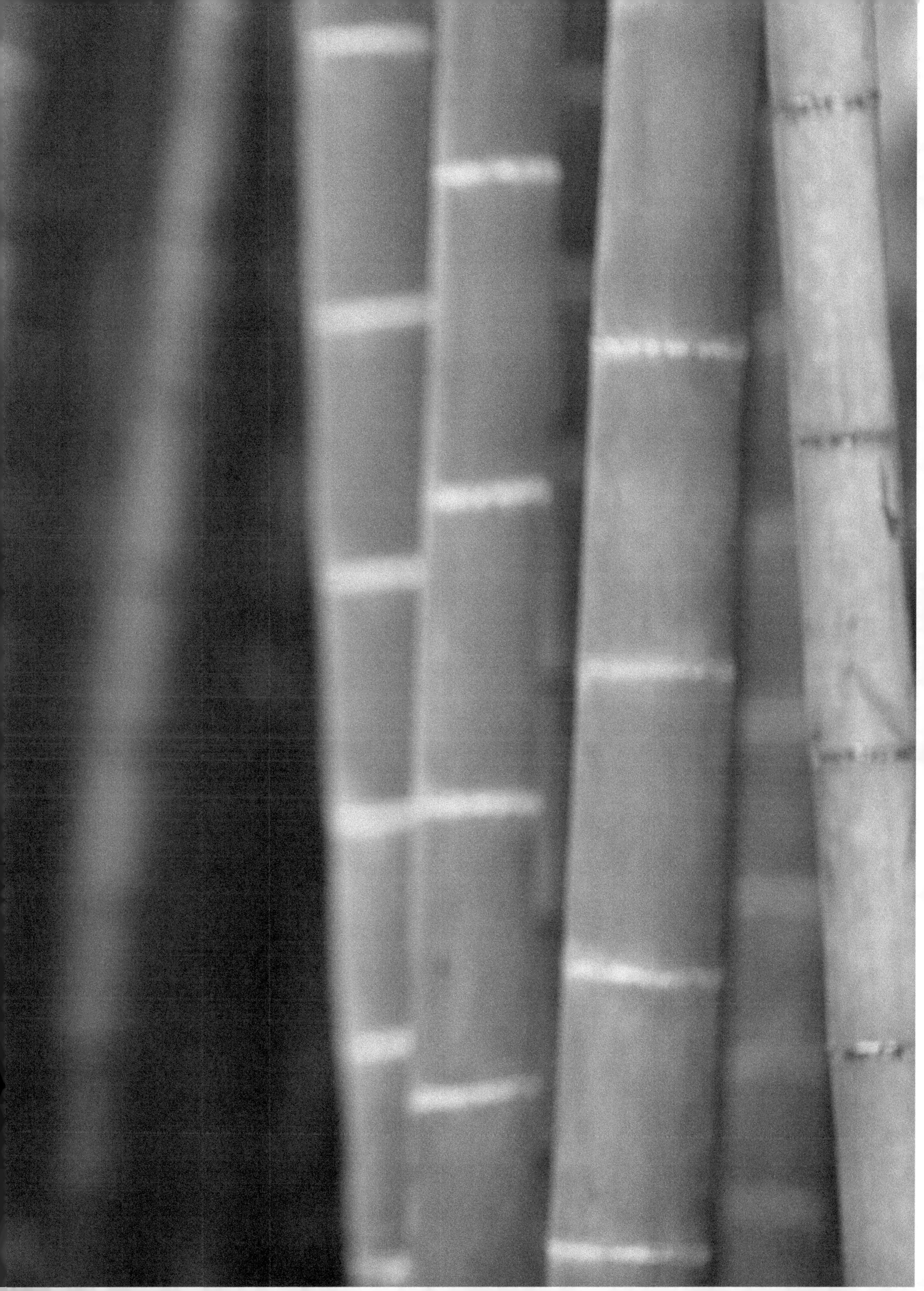

Monk's Cloth	Mulberry Paper	Muslin
Neoprene	Nylon	Oil Cloth
Organza	Ottoman	Oxford
Paint Chip	Panne Velvet	Pearl Paper
Photo Paper	Plush	Poplin
Quilt Batting	Rayon	Satin silk
Spandex	Taffeta	Tissue Paper
Transfer Sheet	Tulle	Tweed
Velour	Velvet	Viscose
Voile	Waffle Cloth	Washi Sheet
Wax Paper	Window Cling	Wool Crepe
Wrapping Paper	True Brushed Paper	Zibeline

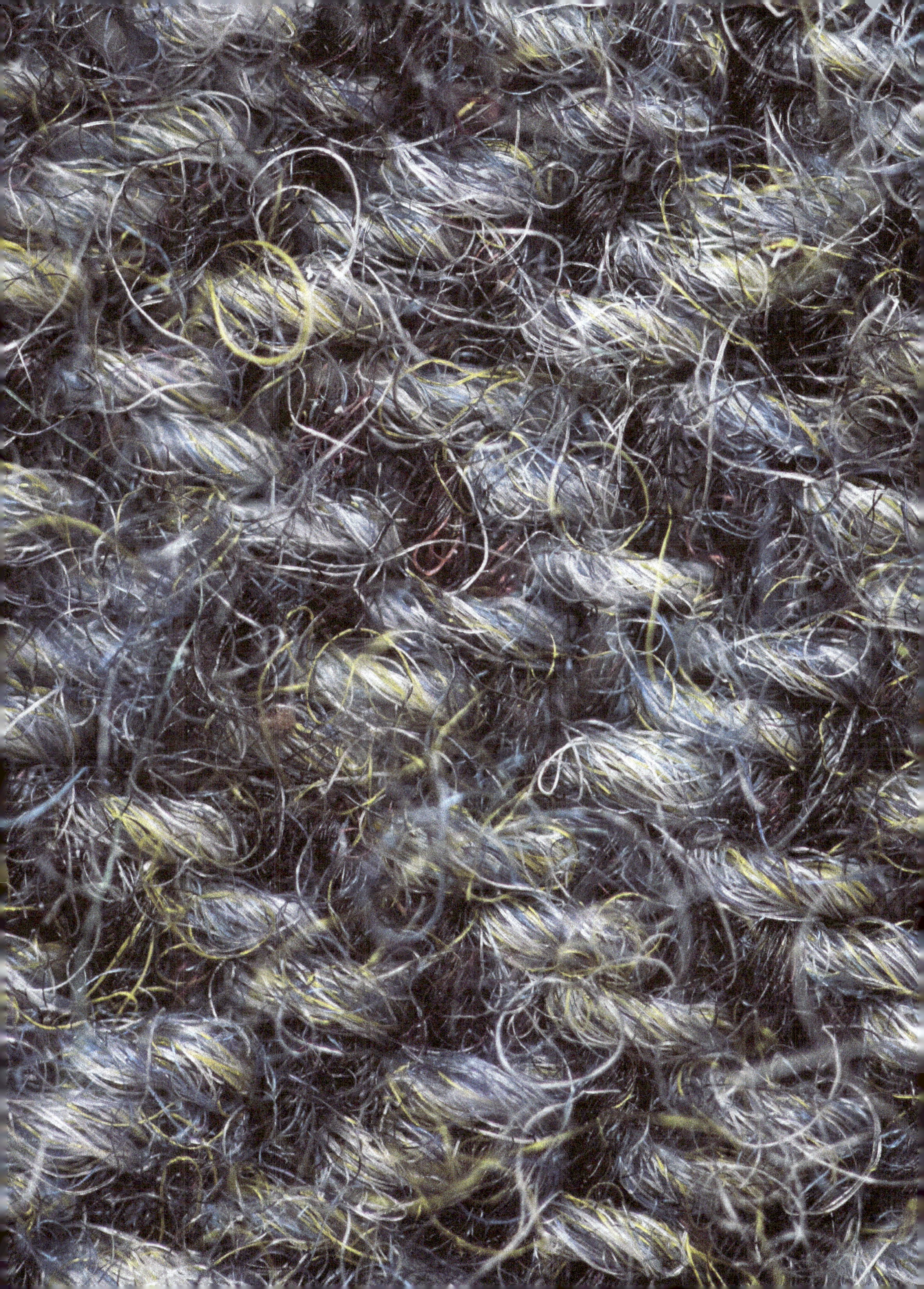

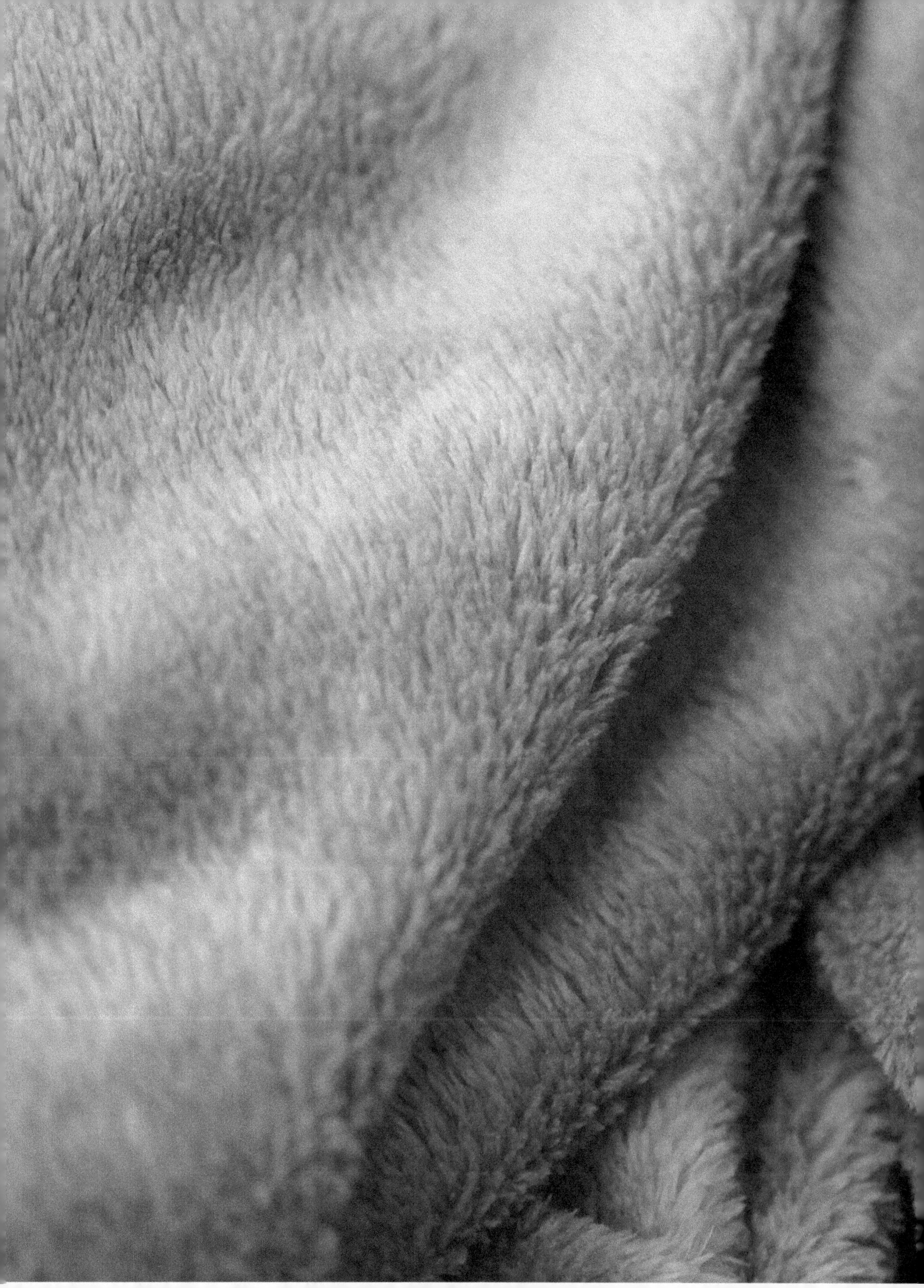

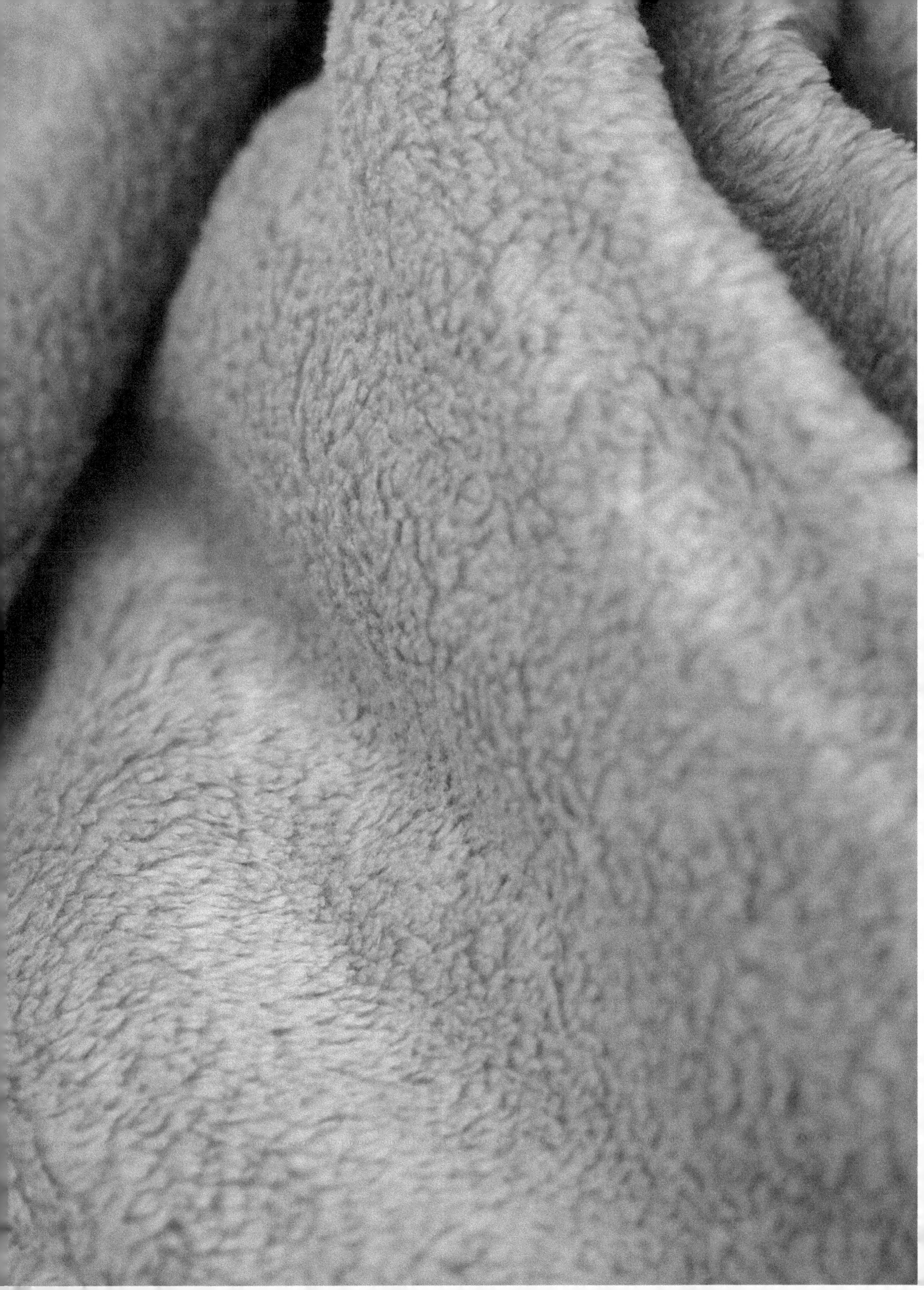

The Cricut Maker can cut anything from felt, leather, and non-bonded fabrics to basswood and balsa wood. Can you see why I'm telling you that you won't need anything else? Of course, new Cricuts will come along and wow us in ways we won't be able to comprehend, but until then, the Cricut Maker is pretty boss. It is also the only Cricut machine with a scoring Stylus and a rotary blade in the box when you make your purchase. It also comes with a calligraphy pen, a fine-point pen, and a washable fabric pen. Minimum additional items are required when purchasing the Cricut Maker.

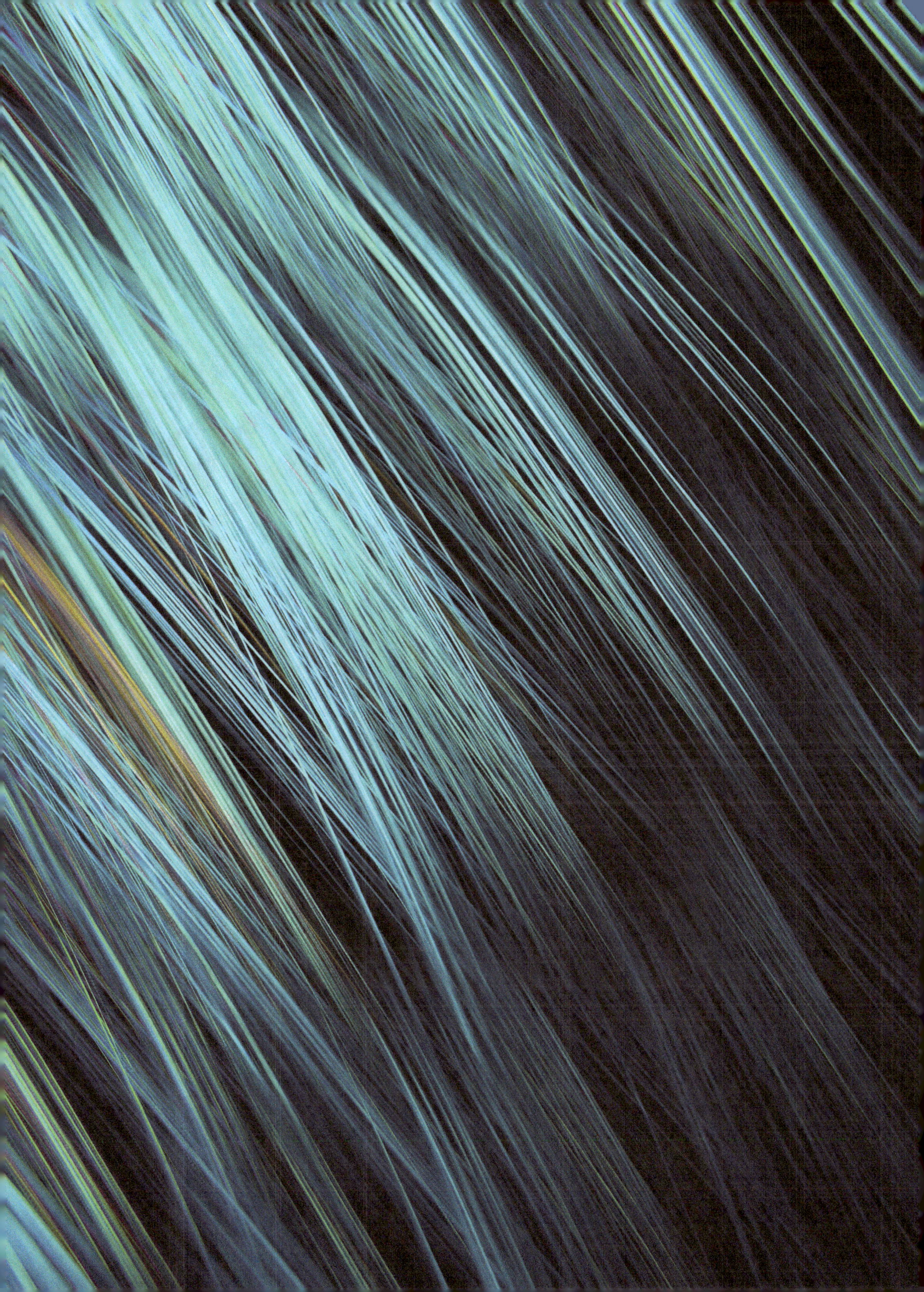

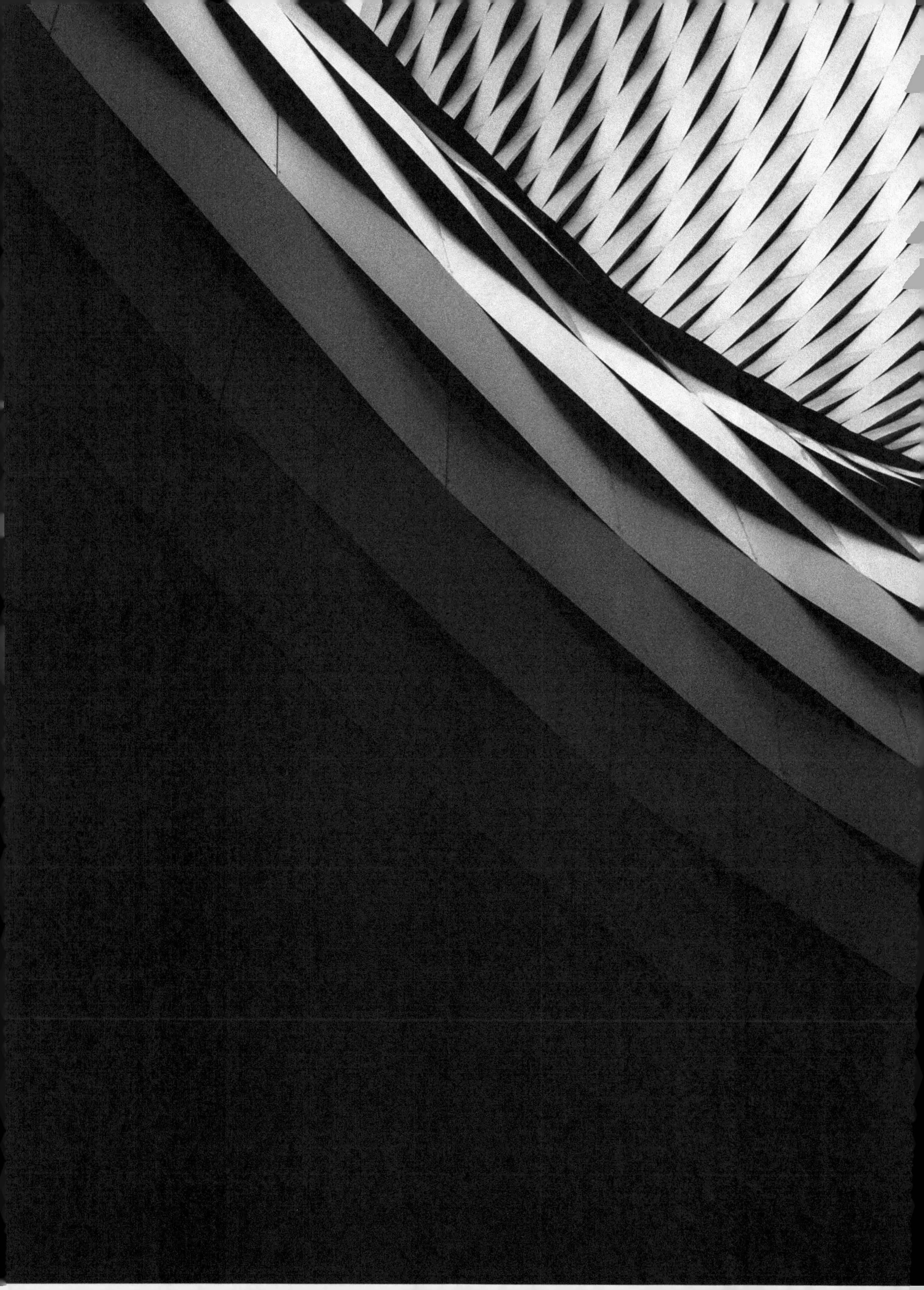

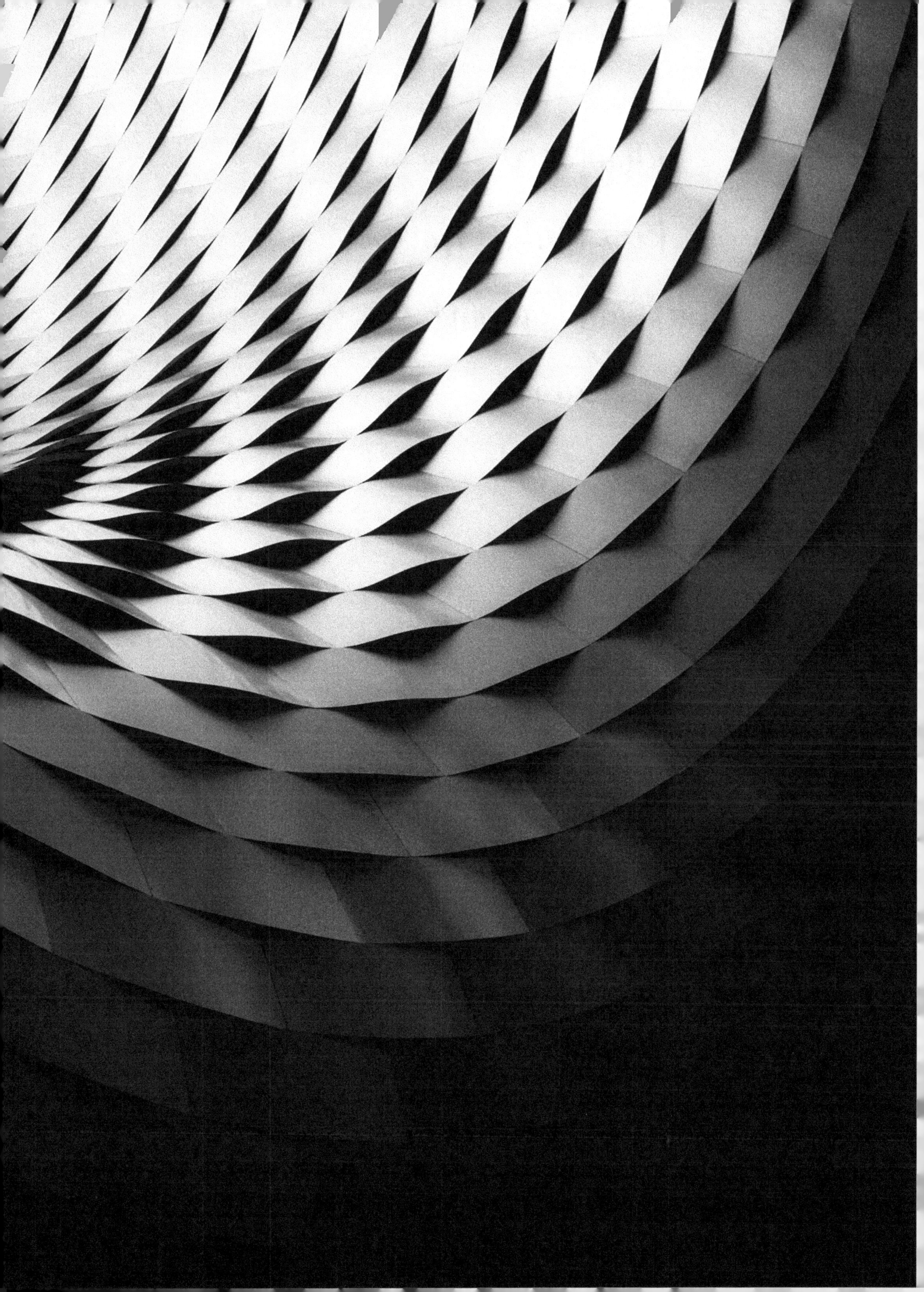

Chapter 5
How to Keep Cricut Maker Machine Clean and Efficient

There are a lot of things which you can achieve by making the correct use of your machine. However, it is not just enough to know these; you need to learn more comfortable and more improved ways to use the device you have acquired. To make the most out of your newly acquired machine, here are a few things you should do;

TEST OUT YOUR MACHINE FIRST

This is a no-brainer, and you should do it as soon as the machine arrives. It is always a safe idea to start by testing out the components of your device and double-checking to ensure that your machine has all the promised accessories. If, at this stage, you discover that your machine is missing a few things, you may want to reach out to membership support immediately and get the issues rectified.

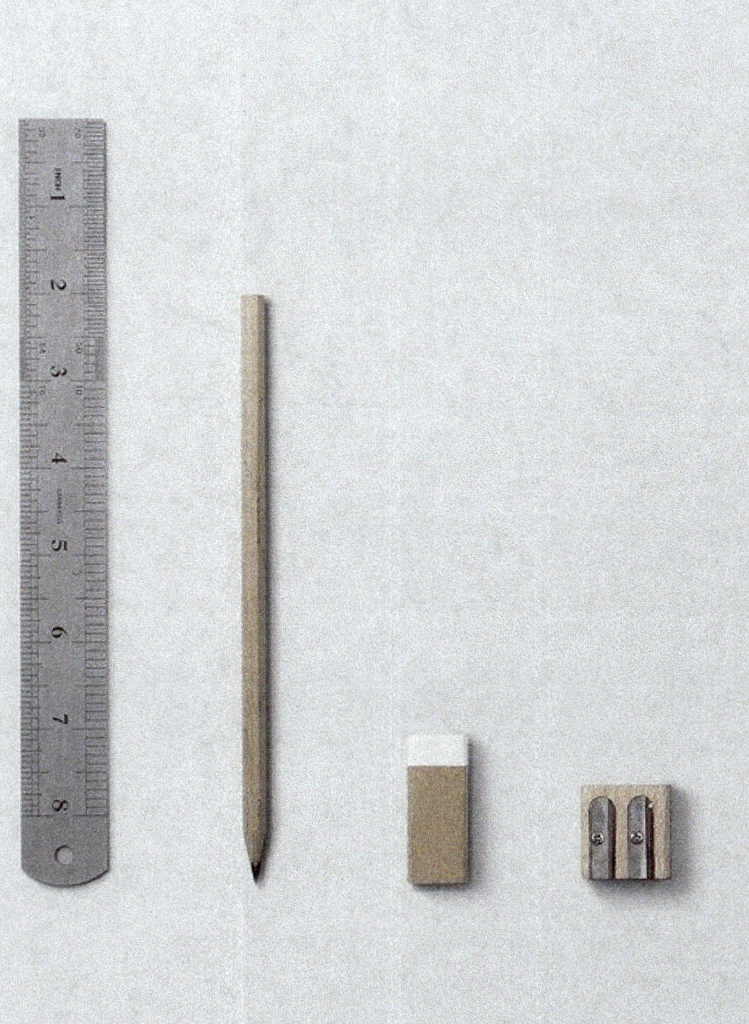

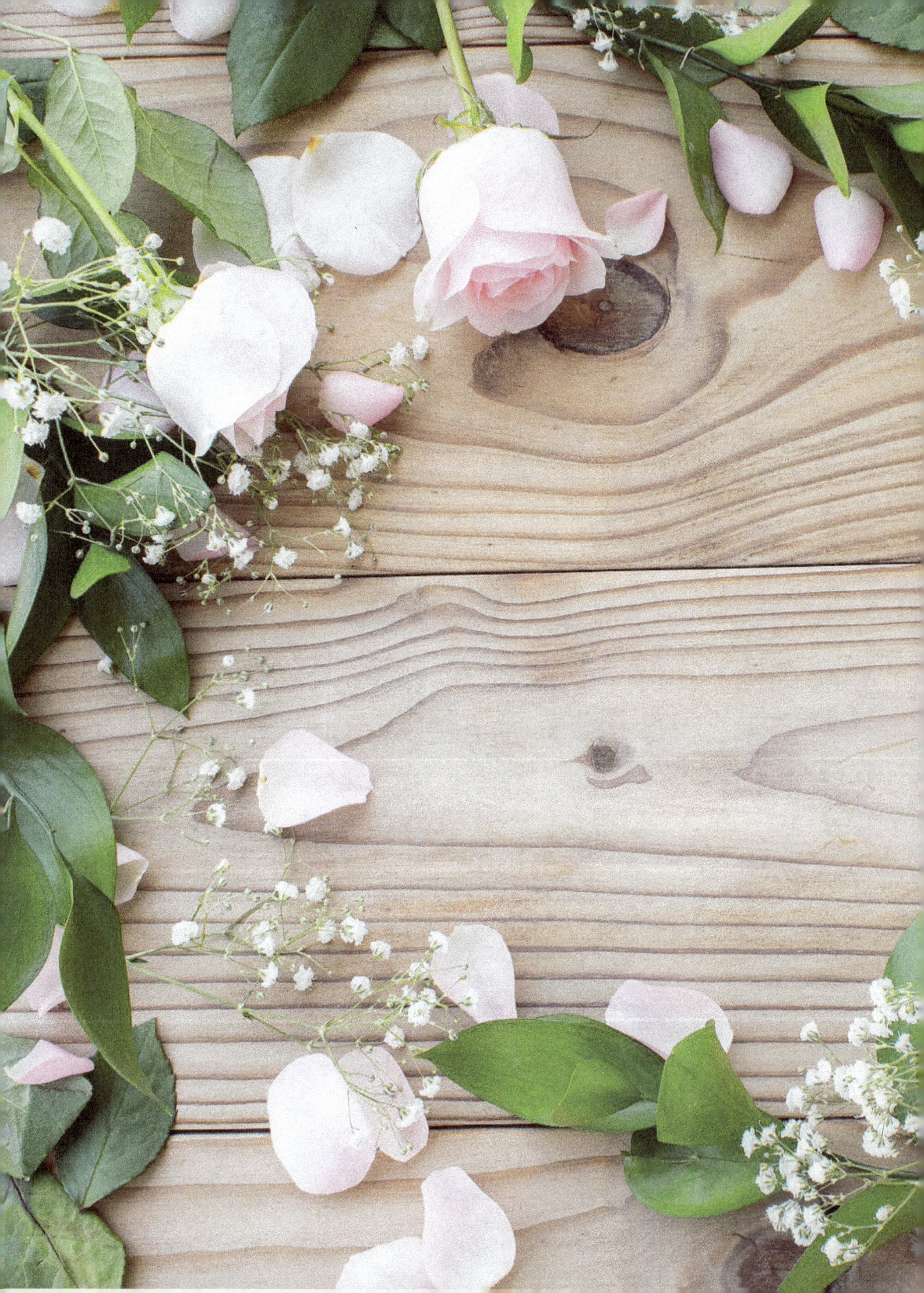

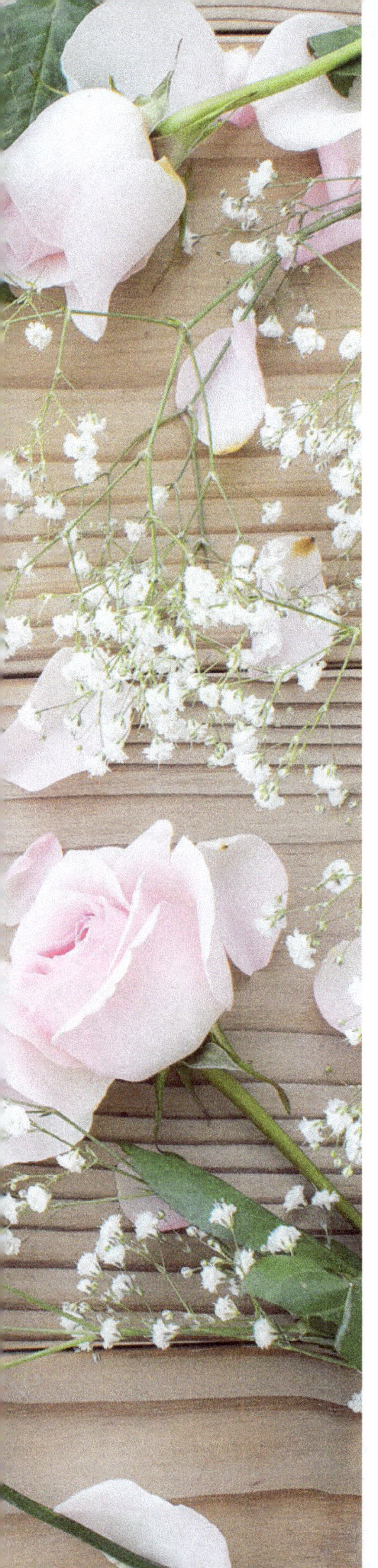

Keep The Components Of Your Machine (Especially The Cutting Mat) Clean

This is one of the parts of the machine that is continuously subjected to wear, tear, attack by dirt, and spoil. To ensure that your device remains in the best of conditions, take out time to clean your mat frequently. Best practices when you are trying to get this done is to make use of a lint roller to wipe down the carpet after every use and to also scan over the mat once you are done with it to make sure that you take out all the little pieces that may remain from the materials you just cut. Also, be sure to frequently replace the plastic protective sheet that came with the mat, and it is not entirely unheard of for you to wash the rug often. However, cleaning the carpet can be a tricky business. Because the mat is meant to be in a specific way, you need to make sure that you wash it so that you do not compromise the integrity of the material the mat is made of. For best practices, wash with lukewarm water and mild dish soap. With these, scrub gently in circular patterns, rinse and allow the mat to drip dry.

Cutting certain materials requires that your mat be a bit sticky to hold the material you are looking to cut in place. Due to some factors like prolonged use, and continuous subjection to heavy work, there may be times that you would need to cut something that requires that the mat has a firm grip on the material, but you may not have access to a good mat that has not lost its stickiness at that time. As a way around this, you can resort to using masking tape or painter's tape to hold the material you are looking to cut in place. However, take this as a cue to change mats because this option won't work forever.

To prevent the confusion that can come from having to deal with many blades that you will need for your different projects. It can be safe to adopt the pattern of storing up your knives so that you can tell almost instantly what blade is used to cut what material. In essence, you need to learn to separate your blades. Let there be blades that you use to cut vinyl, then the ones you use to cut paper, and wood, and all the rest of them. This will ensure that your blades last for much longer and that you don't use the wrong edges for the wrong projects, thereby creating trouble for your new machine. You can get started by finding small jars to hold the blades and then labeling each jar to signify which blades go into it. This way, you do not run the risk of making a mistake with your blade placement.

You do not always have to have the right color of vinyl to embark upon your projects. Let's assume that you are about to get started with a project and you need some green vinyl, but all you have is pink-colored vinyl; you must not get dressed and go off to the mall to get the green-colored ones because there is a way around it. Instead of running off to the mall every time you need a different vinyl color, why not get some Rustoleum Metallic Spray paint for the future. With this, you can give your un-cut vinyl some spraying and color-over without having to spend money every time. Just for a few bucks, you can get this over with.

Dafont.com and 1001freefonts.com are unique

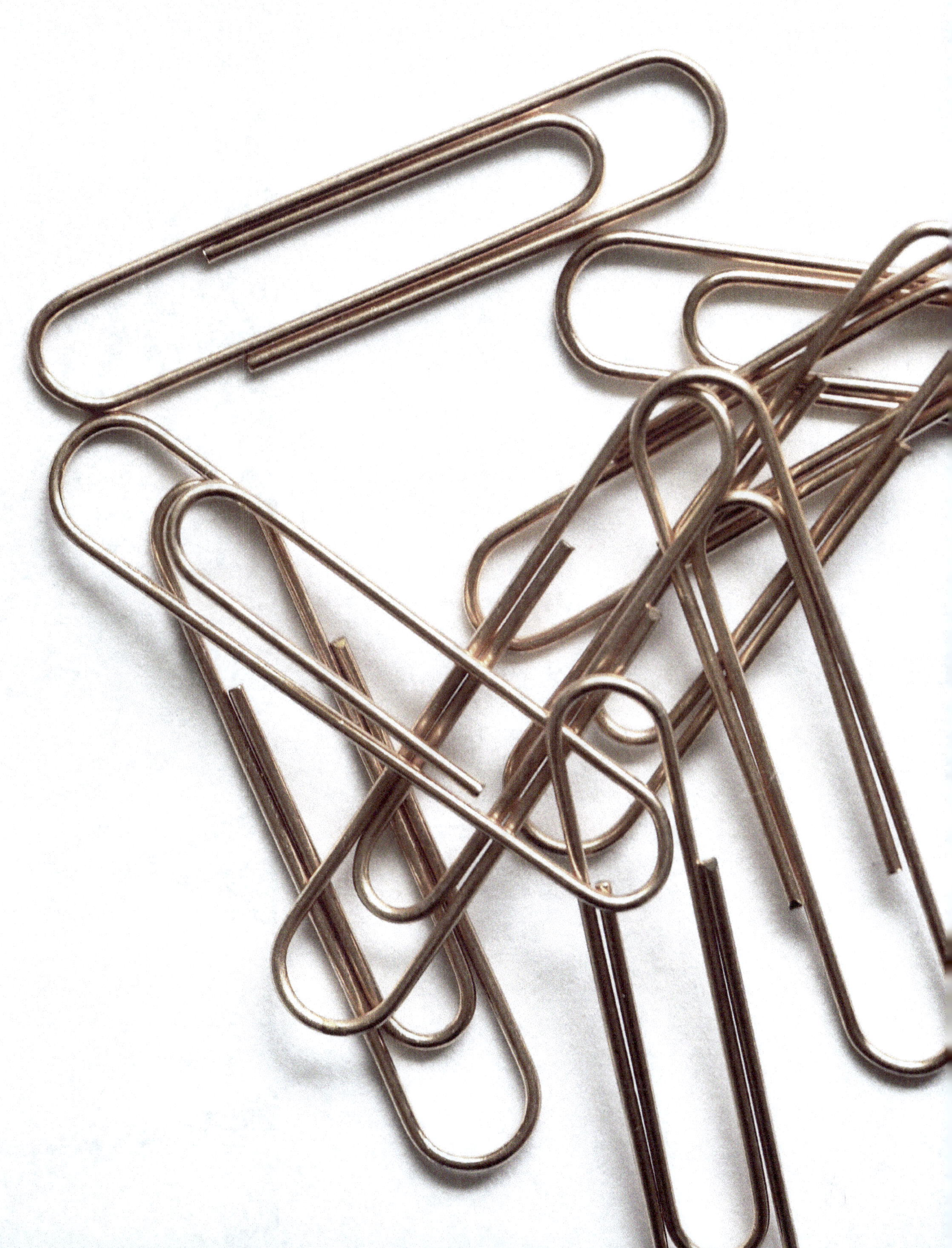

websites where you can find tons of fonts that you can make use of to create even more epic designs. If you have searched through the design space and you have not been able to see something that piques your interests, or you need to try out something new, you may want to visit those platforms and see what they have in store for you. You will also find a lot of support groups on Facebook where you can find a lot of helpful information regarding your creative journey with the machine you have just acquired. Join these groups and be sure to be an active member of them. You will see that some things may bother you that can be a walkover for another person. All you need to do is reach out.

Furthermore, these platforms serve as hosting sites for a ton of helpful tools that can even unclog your creativity even more. Find them as pinned documents, helpful DIY tips, post and comment threads, and in all other formats as they come. The goal is to make sure that you do not try to do this on your own.

Want to do some stenciling, but you are not sure where and how you can get started? There's no need for you to be confused when you can use freezer paper to create custom stencils for your projects. With the Cricut Explore Air 2, you can get to cut the piece and fashion it into some custom-design stencils for your projects.

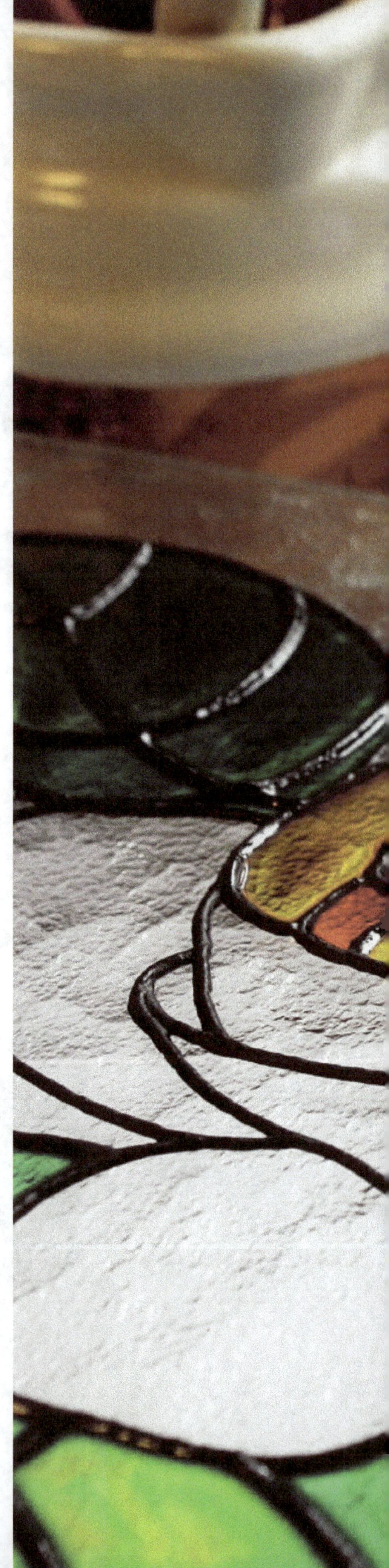

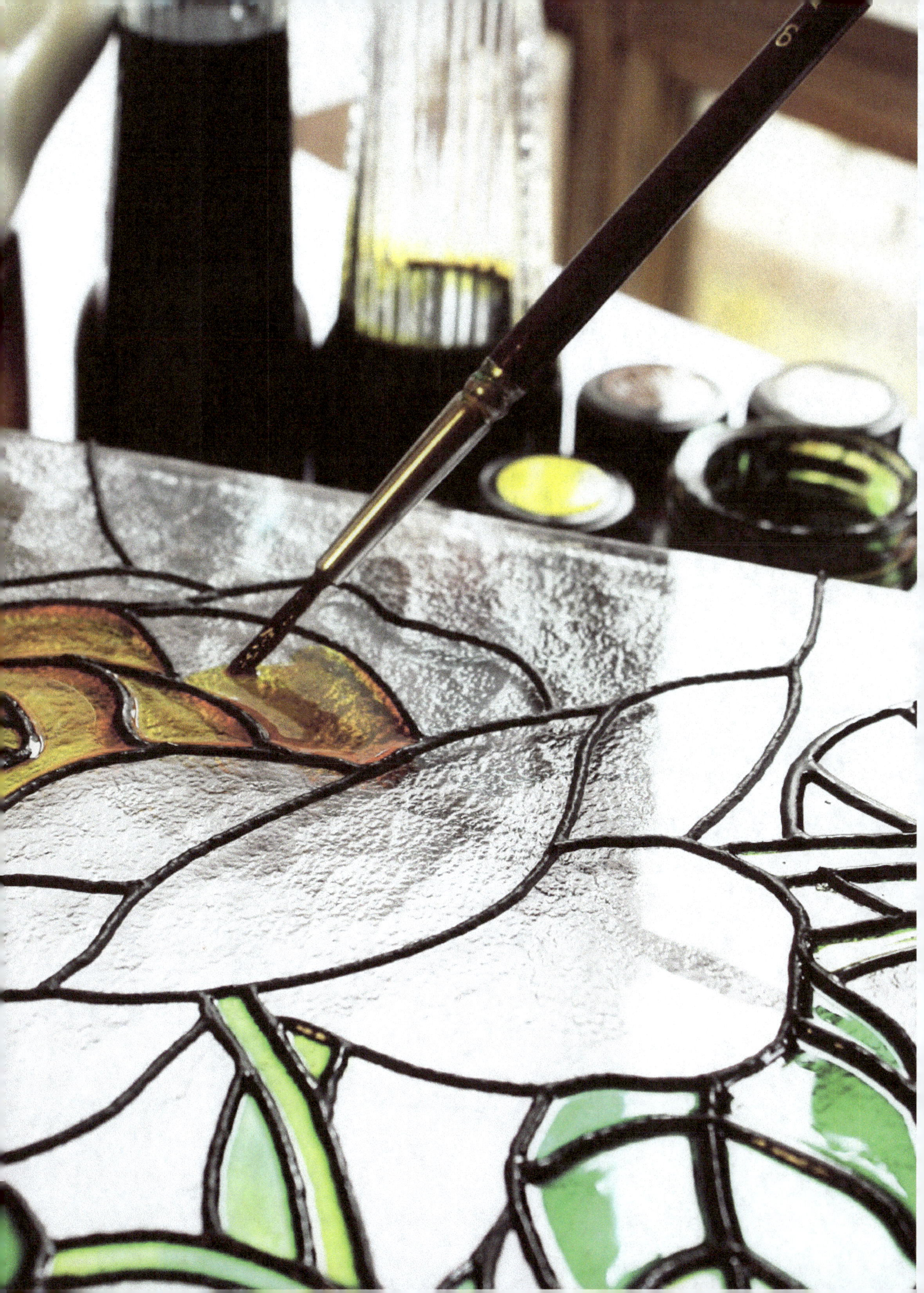

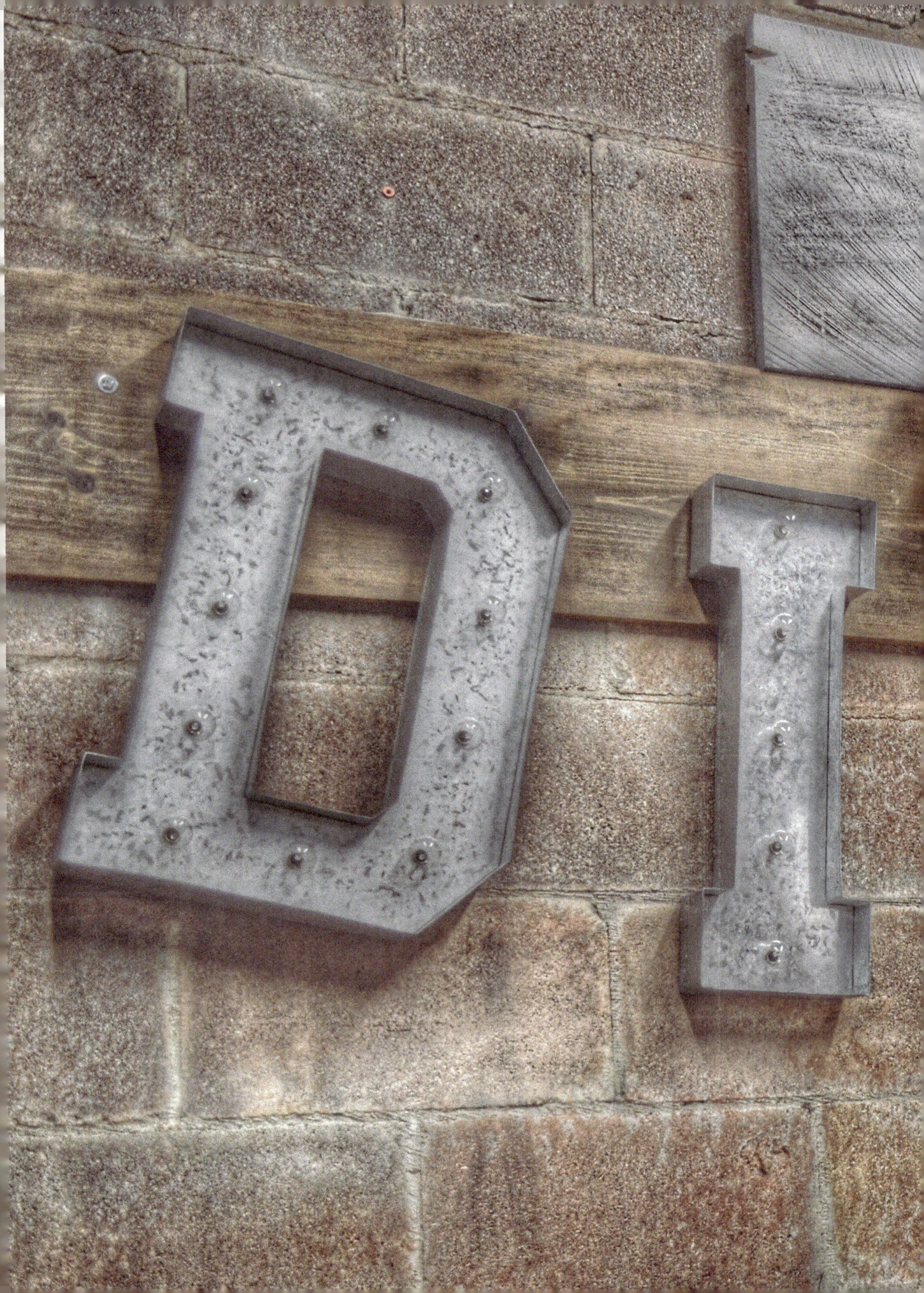

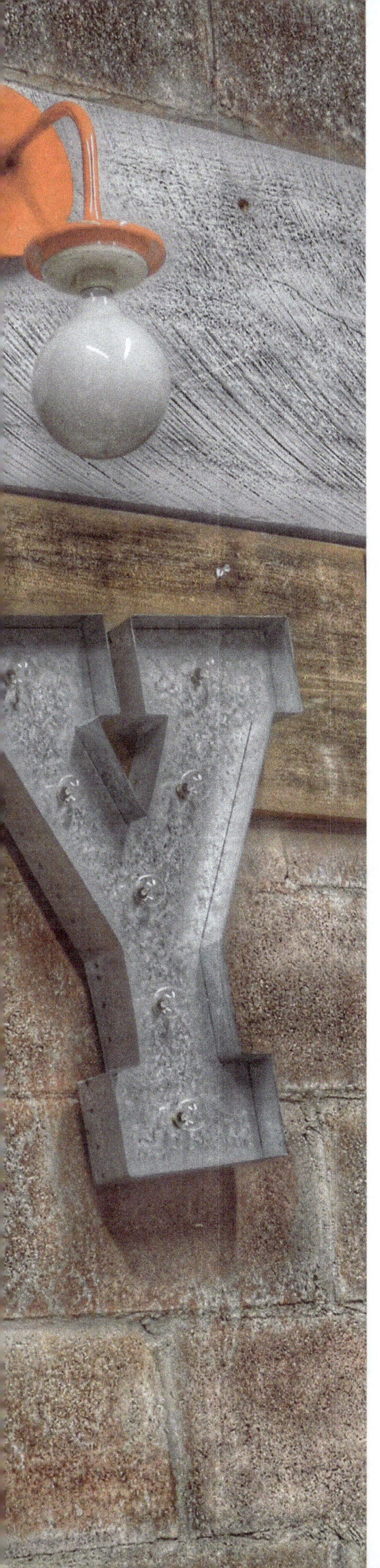

MAKE USE OF TIN FOILS TO SHARPEN YOUR BLADES.

Notwithstanding how careful you are with the blades and how you do not mistake them for cutting different materials, it is not possible for your blades not to get to a point where they become blunt and weak. When your blades get blunt, a great way to get them up and running once again is by making use of tin foils to sharpen them. By pointing with tin foil, you can extend the life of your blade almost by x3. Sharpening is effortless. All you need to do is unclamp the edge and run the blade's tip through the tin foil between 10-15 times.

Using pens other than the Cricut pens to write

Next to the Cricut pens, there are a ton of other brands that you can make use of, even with your machine. They include

Uni-ball Signo UM-153.

Tombow Dual brush pens.

Sakura gelly roll.

By marking and Bic crystal.

Pilot Precise.

The list is endless. The best part is that you can find them online for all these pens, and with just a few dollars, you can have them added to your bucket list of cells to work with. However, to make use of these pens with your machine, you need a pen adapter. Pen adapters work for the Explore Air 2 or newer models of the Cricut machine. With these, you can connect any brand of Cricut pens and draw/write away.

INCREASE YOUR IMAGE OPTIONS BY LEARNING HOW TO MAKE YOUR SVG FILES ONLINE

While the design space and the internet provide you with endless numbers of images, you will agree that there are those times when even the most intricately designed picture does not quite cut it; it does not do justice to what you want to create. Under these circumstances, you need to learn how to bring your inner genius to life.
Using Inkscape, you can create your SVG files from scratch or convert your boring pictures to two-layered SVG files. Inkscape is a free tool that you can use, and making use of it is relatively easy.

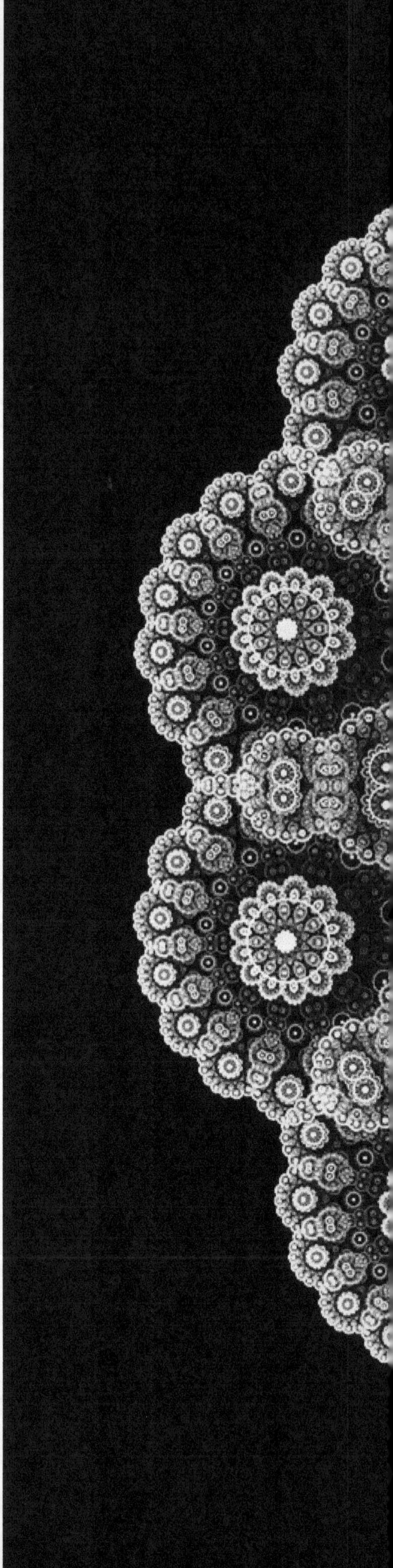

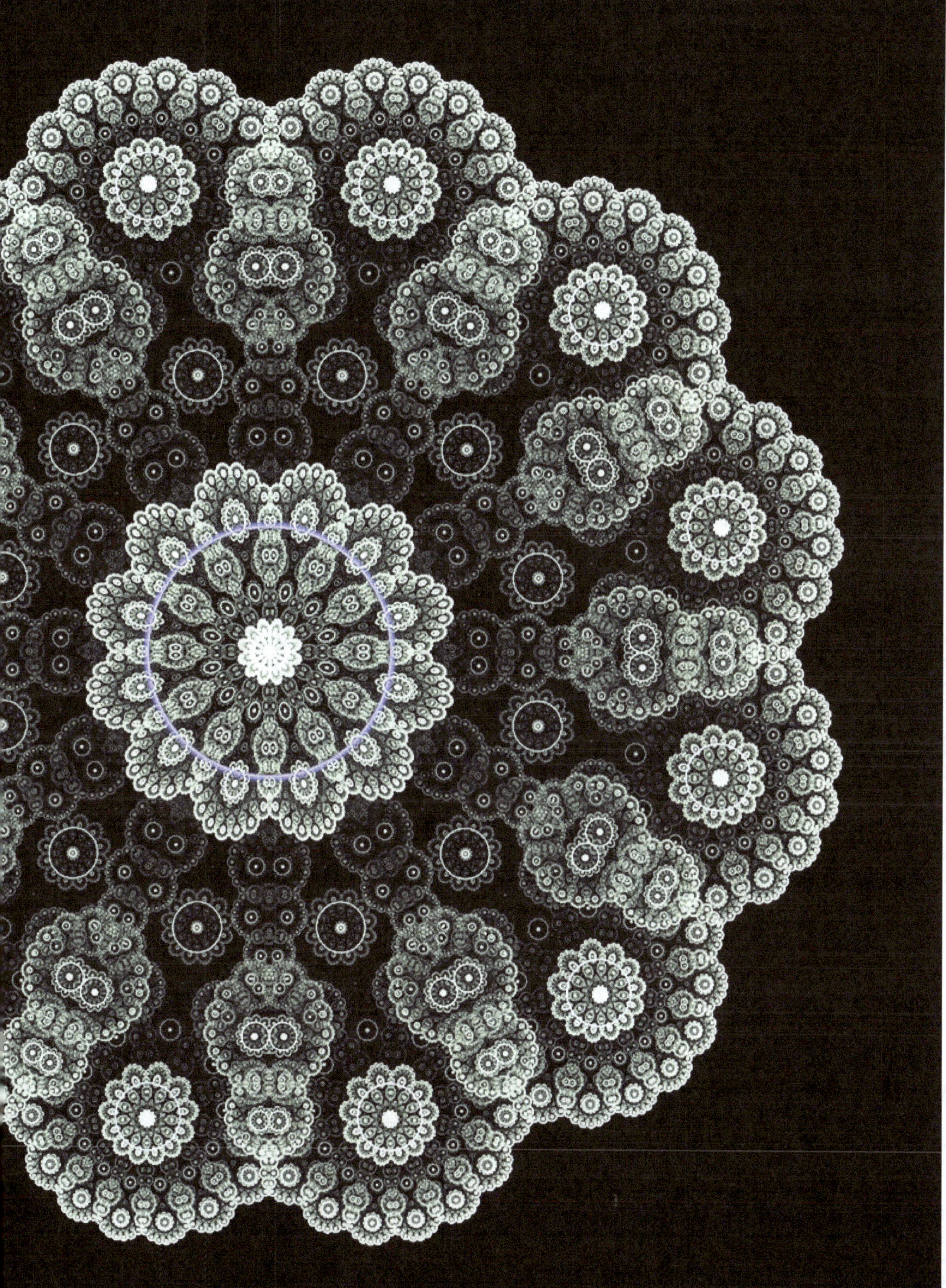

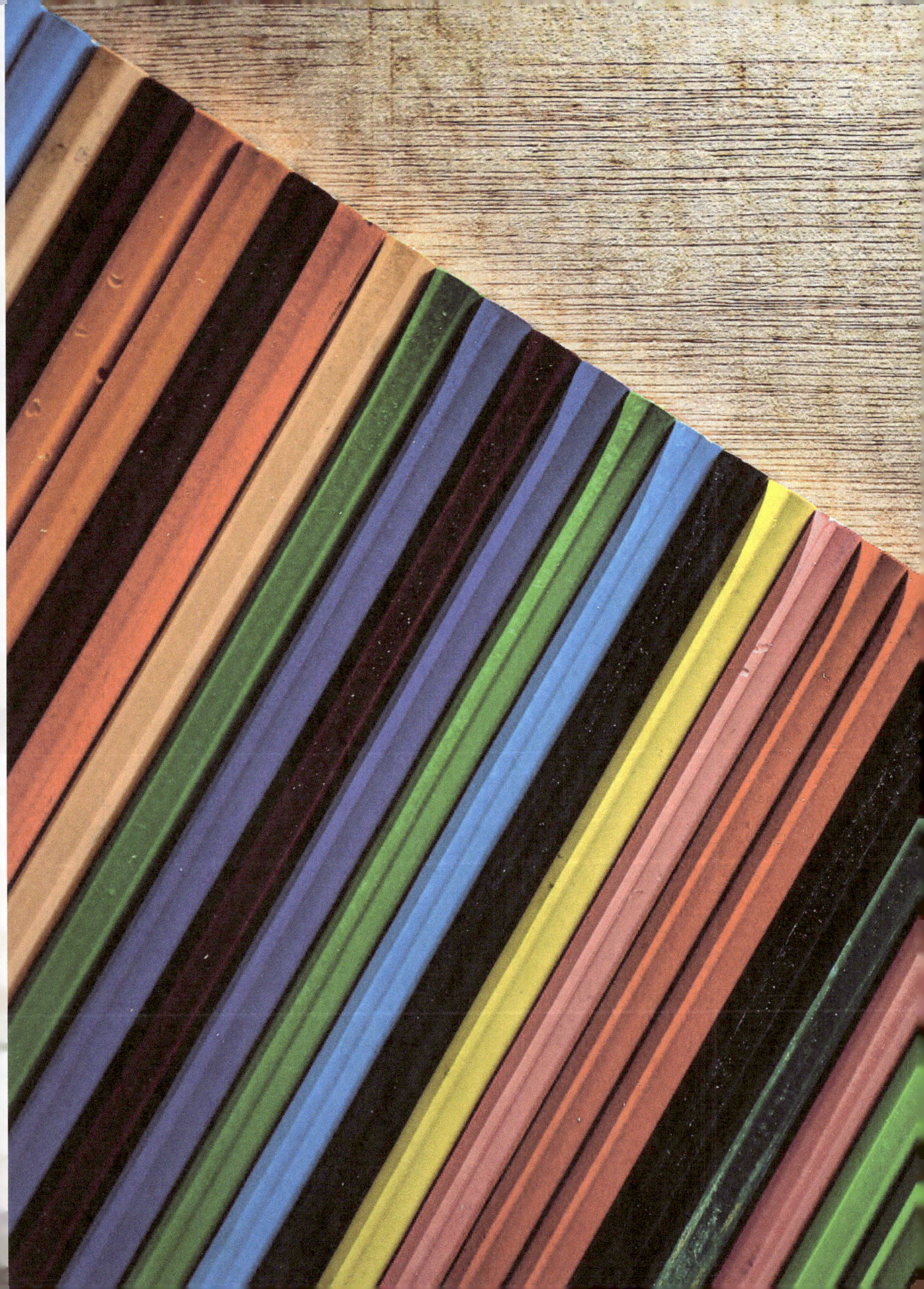

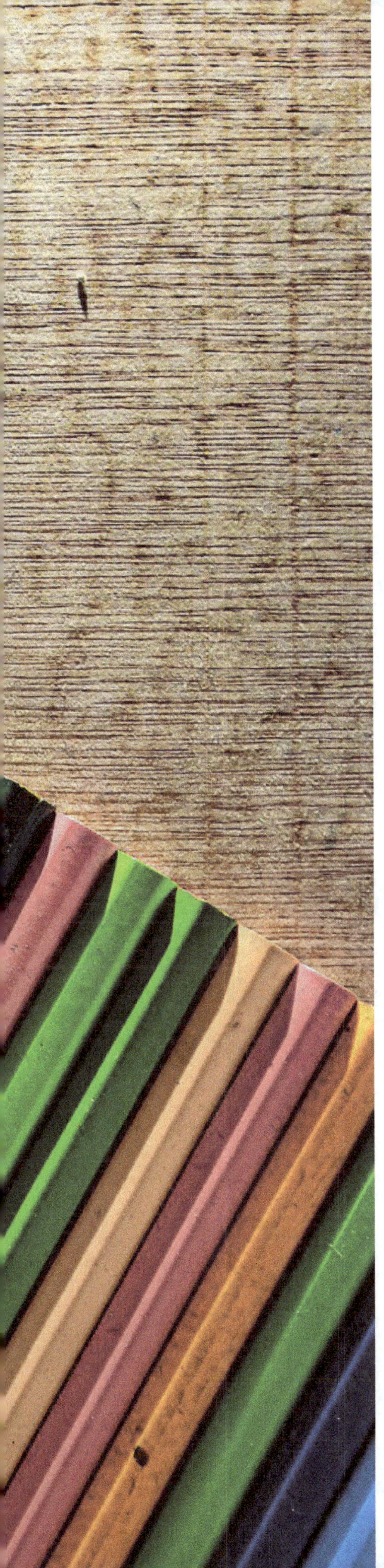

Chapter 6
Common List of Problems with Cricut Maker and How to Solve Them

MATERIAL TEARING OR NOT CUTTING COMPLETELY THROUGH

This is the biggest problem with most Cricut users. When this happens, the image is ruined, and you've wasted material. More machines have been returned or boxed up and put away due to this problem than any other.

But don't panic; if your paper is not cutting correctly, there are several steps you can take to try and correct the problem.

Most important is this: Anytime you work with the blade, TURN YOUR MACHINE OFF. I know it's easy to forget this because you're frustrated, and you're trying this and that to make it work correctly. But this is a necessary safety precaution that you should remember.

Make simple adjustments at first. Turn the pressure down one. Did it help? If not, turn the blade down one number. Also, make sure the mat is free of debris so the edge rides smoothly.

Usually, the thicker the material, the higher the pressure number should be cut through the paper. Don't forget to use the multi-cut function if you have that option. It may take a little longer to cut 2, 3, or 4 times, but it should cut clean through by then.

For those of you using the smaller bugs that do not have that option, here is how to make your own multi-cut function. After the image has been cut, don't unload the mat. Just hit load paper, repeat last, and cut. You can repeat this sequence 2, 3, or 4 times to ensure your image is completely cut out.

If you are using thinner paper and it is tearing, try reducing the pressure and slowing down the speed. When cutting intricate designs, you have to give the blade enough time to maneuver through the procedure. By slowing it down, it will be able to make cleaner cuts.

Clean the blade's edge to be sure no fuzz, glue, or scraps of paper are stuck to it.

Make sure the blade is installed correctly. Take it out and put it back, so it's seated firmly. The edge should be steady while it's making cuts. If it makes a shaky movement, it's not installed correctly, or there's a problem with the blade housing.

Be aware that there is a deep cutting blade for thicker material. You'll want to switch to this blade when you're cutting heavy card stock. This will also save wear and tear on your regular knife. Missing a lot of thick material will wear your blade out quicker than thinner material and cause you to change it more often.

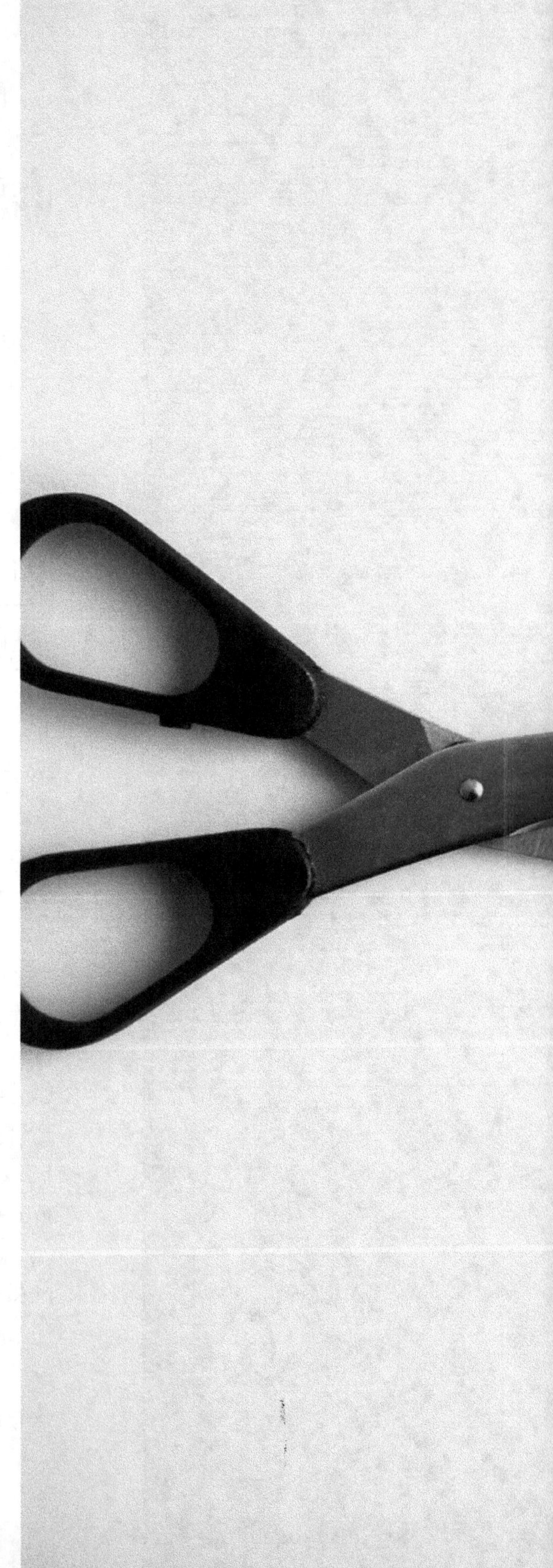

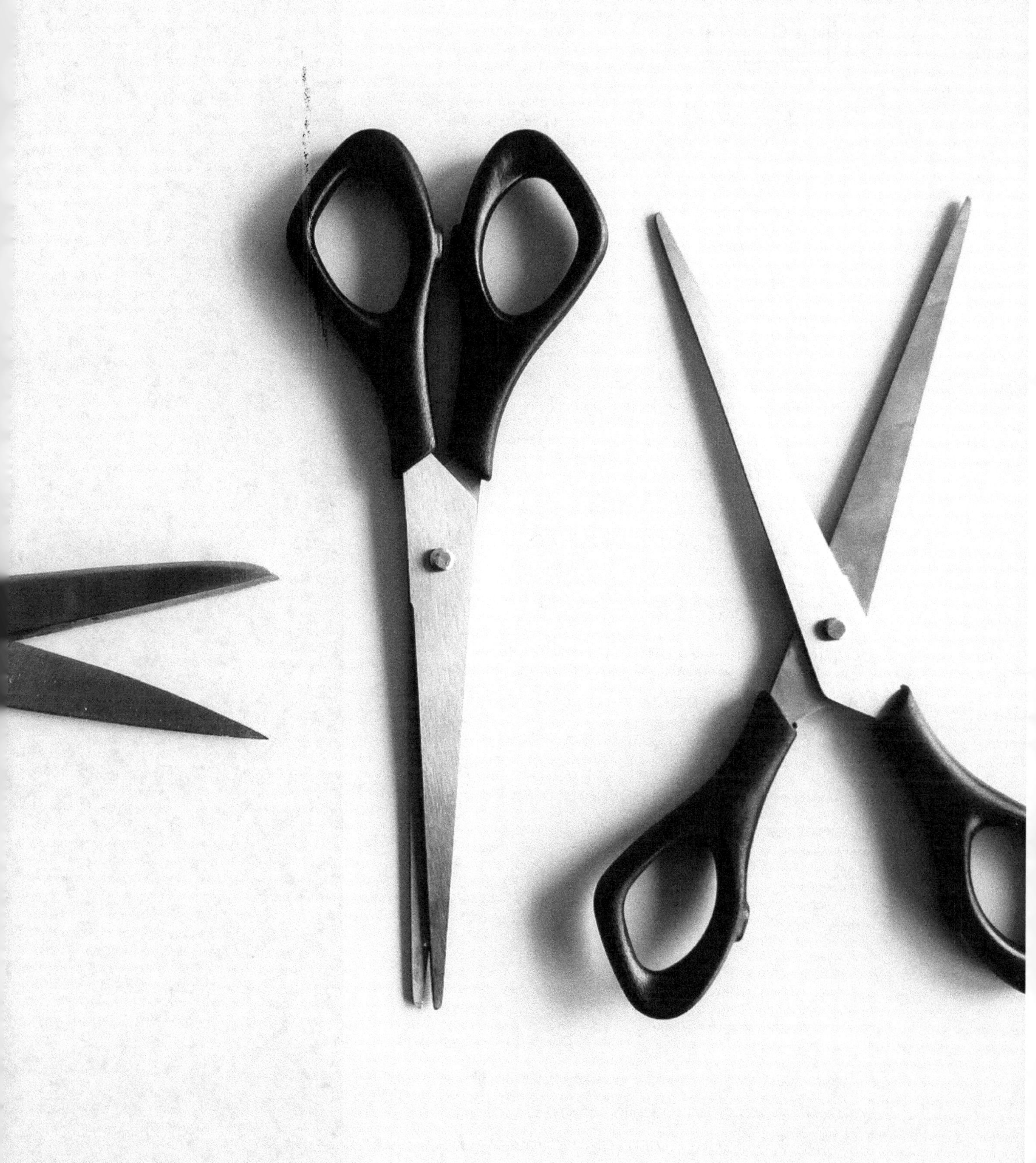

MACHINE FREEZING

Remember always to turn your machine off when you switch cartridges. When you change cartridges, leaving the device on, it's called "hot-swapping," It can sometimes cause the engine to freeze. This is more of an issue with the older models and doesn't seem to apply to Expression 2.

You know how quirky electronic gadgets can be, so give your machine rest for five or ten minutes every hour. If you work for several hours continuously, your machine might overheat and freeze up.

Turn the machine off and take a break. Restart it when you come back, and it should be fine. Then remember not to rush programming the device and give it an occasional rest.

Don't press a long list of commands quickly. If you give it too much information too fast, it will get confused in the same way a computer sometimes does and freeze up. Instead of typing in one long phrase, try dividing up your words into several cuts.

If you're using special feature keys, make sure you press them first before selecting the letters.

POWER PROBLEMS

If you turn your machine on and nothing happens, the power adapter may be at fault. Jiggle the power cord at the outlet and

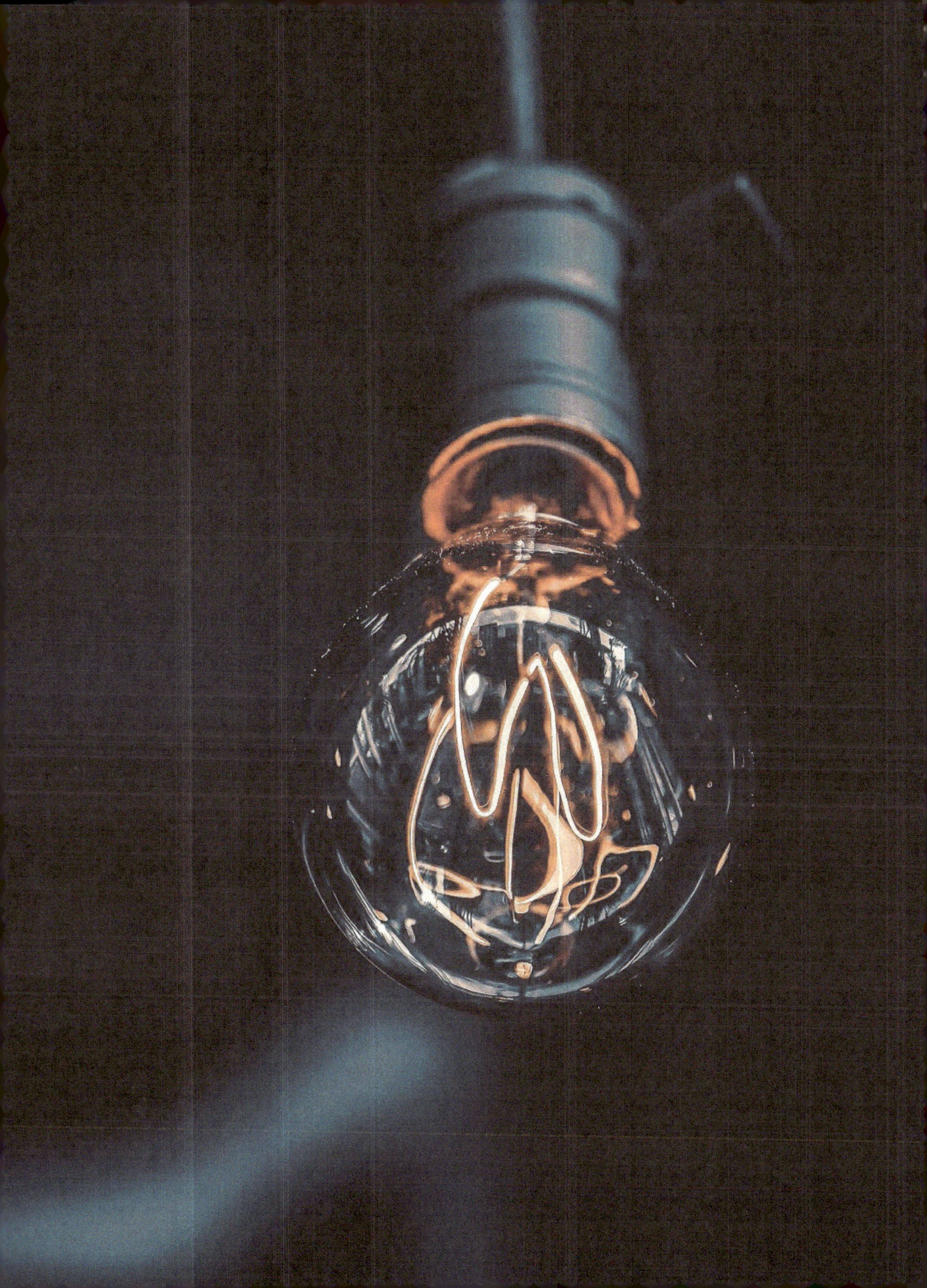

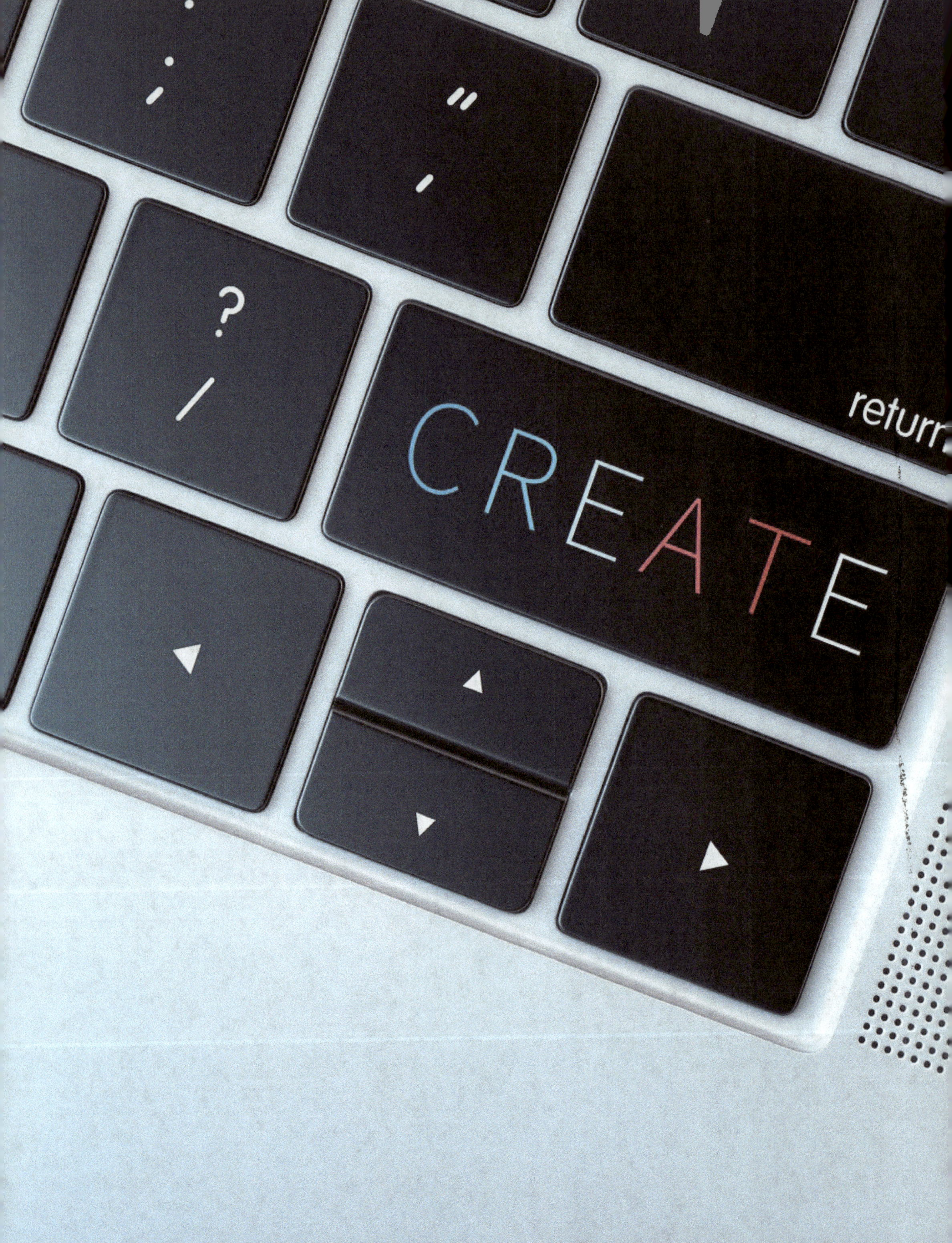

where it connects to the device to make sure it's firmly attached. Ideally, you want to test the adapter before buying a new one. Swap cards with a friend and see if that fixed the problem. Replacement adapters can be found on eBay by searching for Cricut adapter power supply.

The connection points inside the machine may also pose a problem; here is how to test that. Hold down the plug where it inserts into the back of the device and turn it on. If it powers up, then the problem is inside the machine, and the connection points will have to be soldered again.

If the machine powers up but will not cut, then try a hard reset.

Here are a few tips. Have you turned on your machine, you watch it light up and hear it gearing up, but when you try to cut, nothing happens? Or you're stuck on the welcome screen, or the LCD screen is unresponsive.

Well, here are two quick fixes to try. First, try a hard reset, sometimes called the rainbow screen to reset to recalibrate your die cutter. If that does not resolve the problem, you're going to have to restore the settings.

To help cut down on errors, try to keep your machine updated. When an update is available, you should receive a message encouraging you to install the latest version.

For those of you using third-party software that is no longer compatible with the Cricut, you probably already know that updating your machine may disable that software.

When you cut heavy paper, and your machine shuts down, try switching to the standard paper setting and use the multi-cut function.

CARRIAGE WILL NOT MOVE

If the carriage assembly does not move, check to see if the belt has broken or if the car has fallen off the track. Provo Craft does not sell replacement parts, which is nuts, so try to find a compatible belt at a vacuum repair shop.
If the wheels have fallen off the track, remove the plastic cover and look for a tiny screw by the wheel unscrew it. You now should be able to move the wheel back on track.

UNRESPONSIVE KEYBOARD

If you are sure you are pressing the keys firmly, you have a cartridge inserted correctly and a mat loaded ready to go, but the keypad is still not accepting your selection; the problem may be internal. You will have to remove the keyboard and check if the display cable is connected to the keypad and the motherboard. If the connections are secure, you have a circuit board problem, and repairs are beyond this book's scope.
An important reminder, please do not attempt any repairs unless your machine is out of warranty.

WEIRD LCD SCREEN

The LCD screen is now showing strange symbols or is blank after doing a firmware update. Try rerunning the update, making sure your selections are correct.

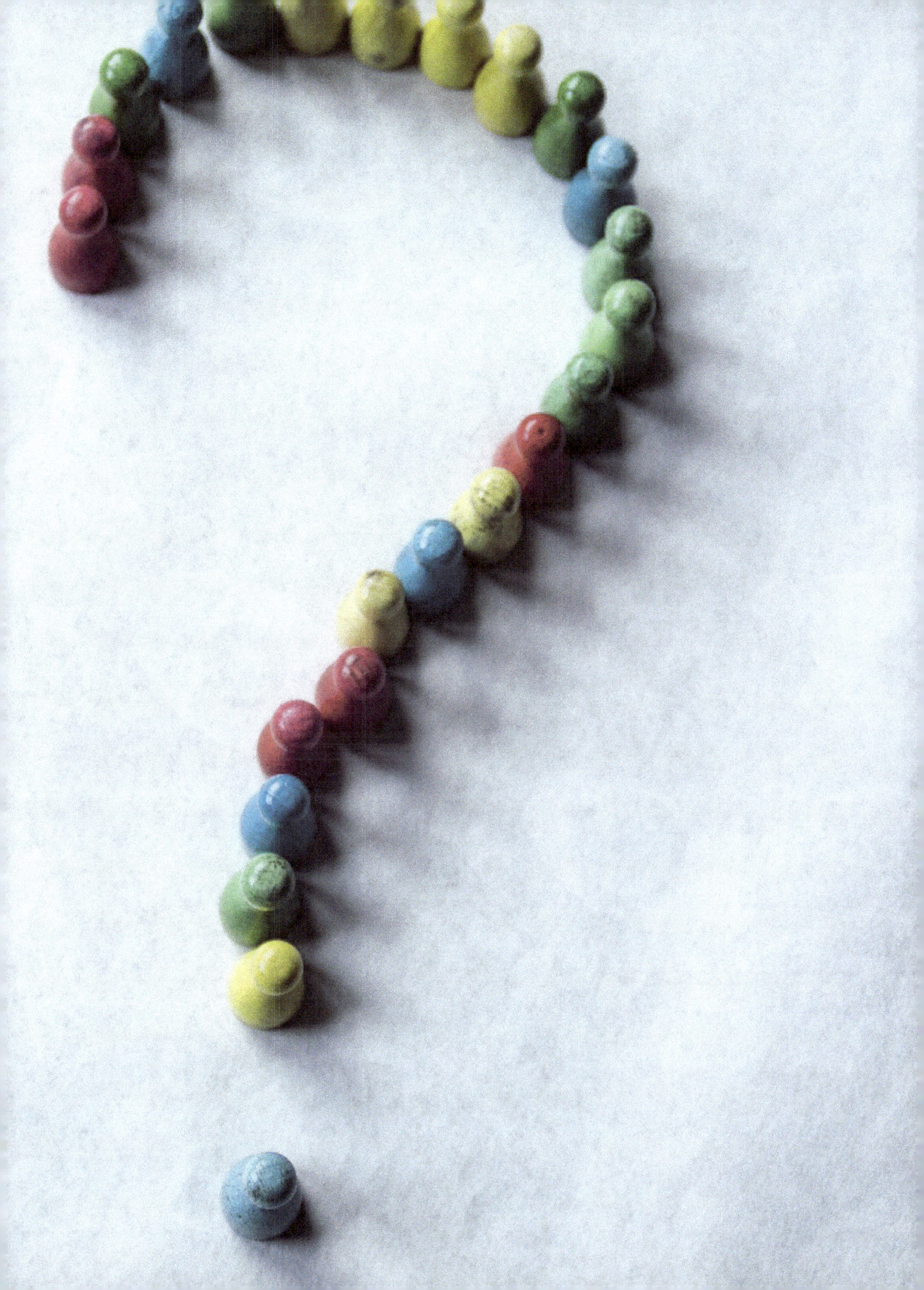

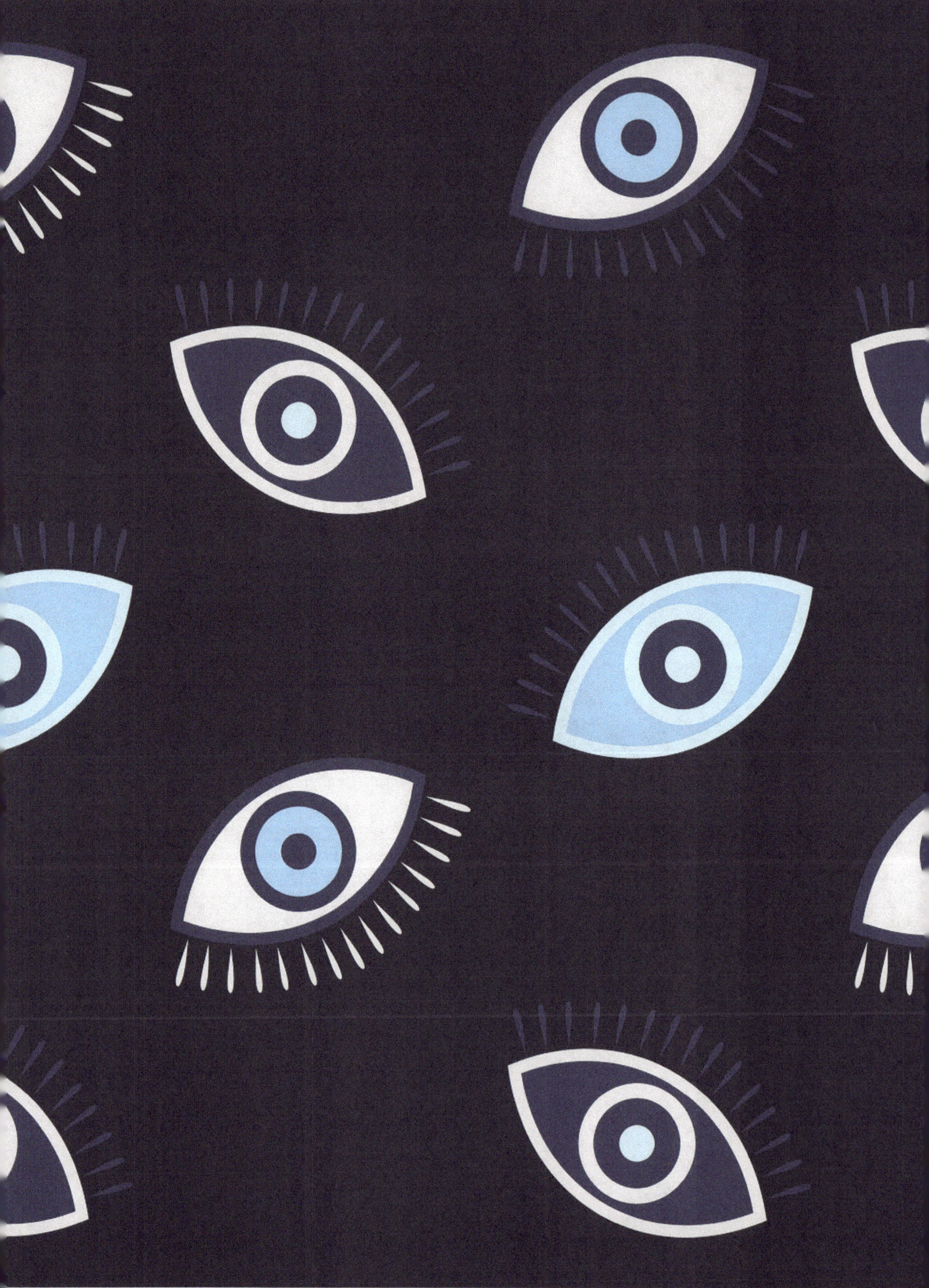

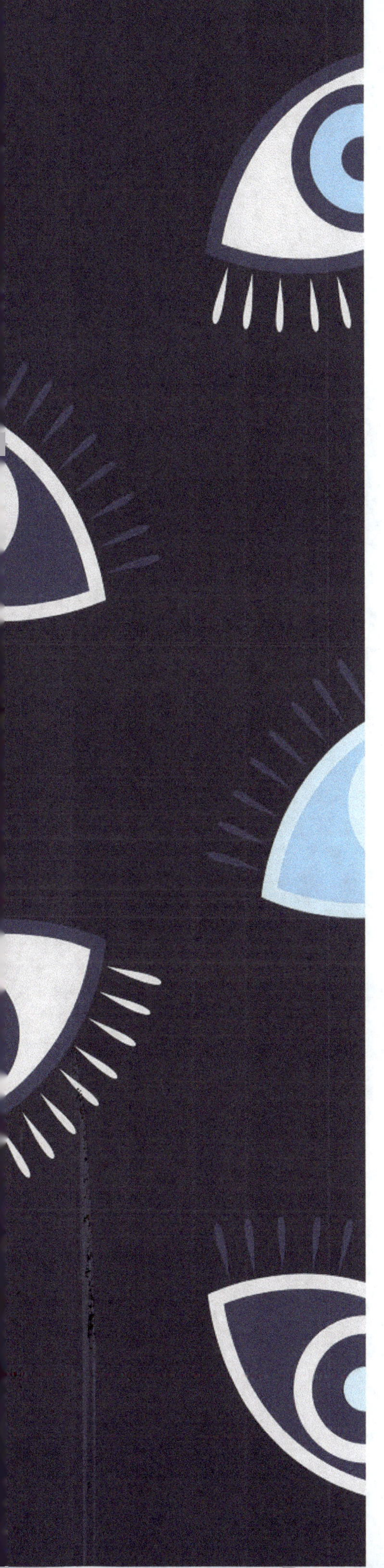

When the image you choose is more significant than the mat or paper size you selected, the preview screen will look grayed out instead of showing the picture. So, increase the paper and mat size or decrease the size of your image.

Also, watch out for the gray box effect when using the center point feature. Move the start position down until you see the image appear. The same thing may happen when using the fit to length feature. Try changing to landscape mode and shorten the length size until the image appears.

Occasionally using the undo button will cause the preview screen to turn black; unfortunately, the only thing to do is turn the machine off. Your work will be lost, and you have to start again.

CARTRIDGE ERRORS

Sometimes dust or debris accumulates in the cartridge port gently blows out any paper fiber that may have collected in the opening. Make sure the contact points are clean and that nothing is preventing the cartridge from being read correctly.

With any electrical machine, overheating can be a problem. If you get a cartridge error after using your device for a while, turn it off and let it cool down for about fifteen minutes.

If this is the first time you're using the cartridge, and you get an error, I'm sure you know the trick about turning the cartridge around and inserting it backward.

If you thought you could use your Imagine cartridges with your Expression 2, think again. You will get an error message because you can only use the art cartridges you can cut with; the colors and patterns cartridges are for printing.

Even brand-new items fresh out of the box can be defective. If you see a cartridge error 1, 2, 3, 4, 5, 6, 9, or 99, call customer service and tell them the name, serial number, and error message number, and they may replace the cartridge.

TROUBLE CONNECTING TO YOUR COMPUTER

All Cricut machines come with a USB cord that lets you connect to your computer and use the other products like the Cricut Design Studio software, Cricut Craft Room, or the Cricut Gypsy with your machines.

Double-check your USB connection and try another port.

Check to see if you may have a firewall or antivirus software that is blocking the connection. See if you're running the latest firmware. You may need to update. Older machines update via firmware (Personal Cutter, Expression, Create, and Cake) the newer (Expression 2, Imagine, and Gypsy) use the Sync program to update.

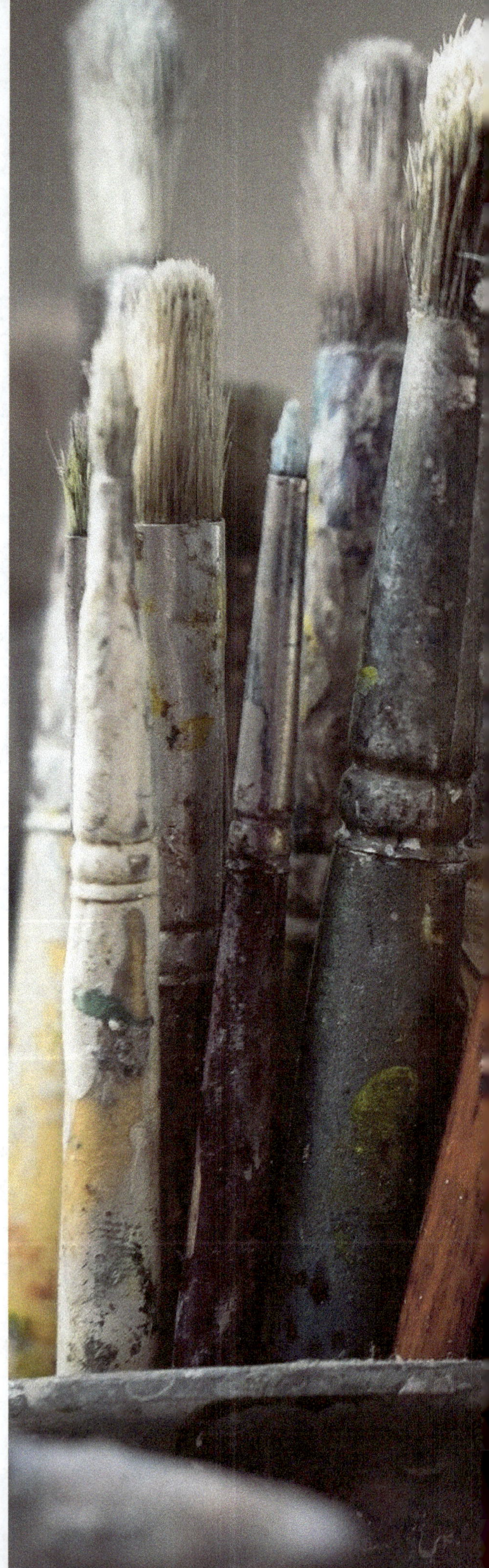

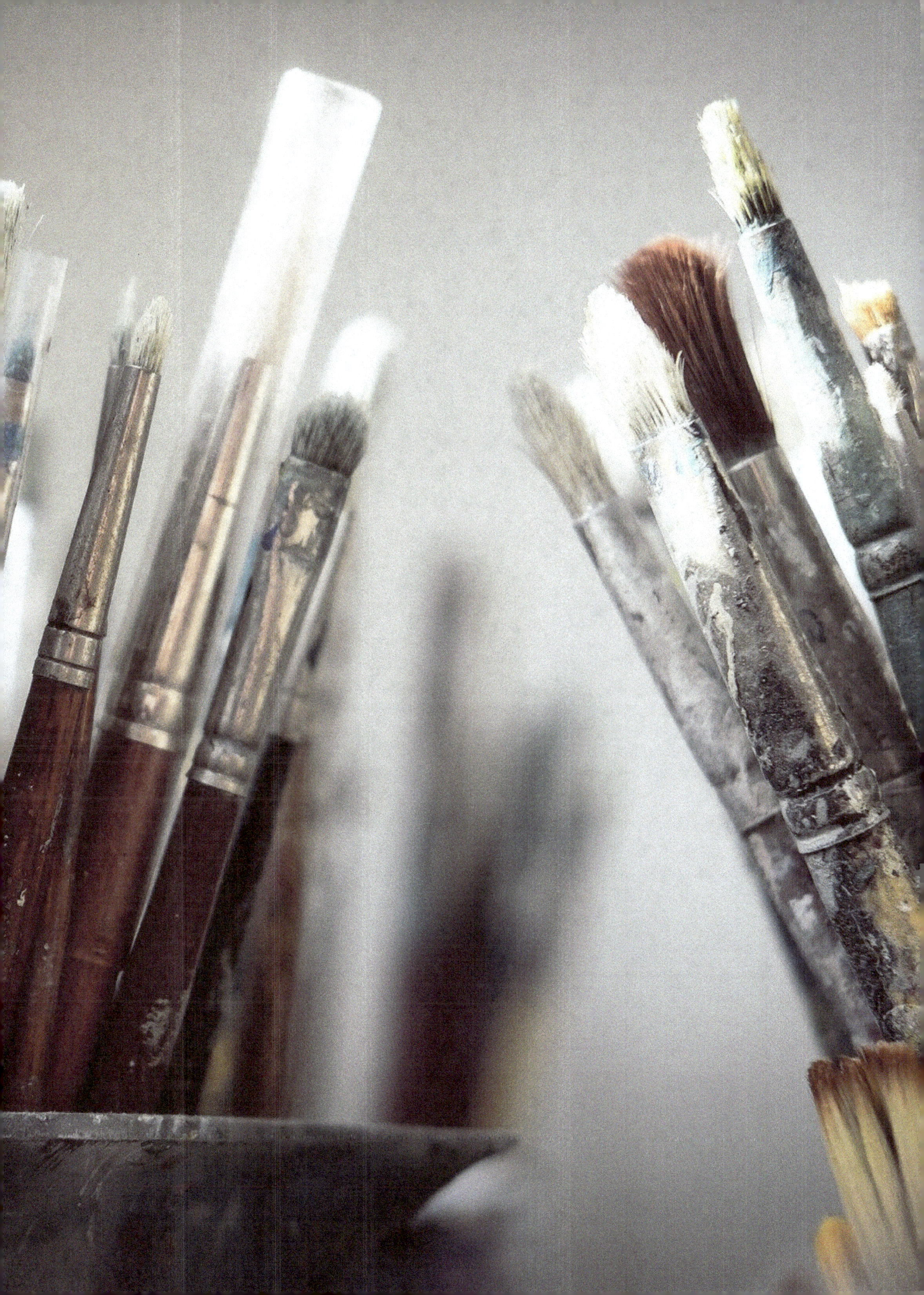

Conclusion

It's time to get crafting! Enjoy your new knowledge of your fantastic machine and give a new project a try. The beauty of the Cricut is the versatility of functions and user-friendly format. Use this to make your life and home and those of your friends and family more exciting and beautiful!

Using a Cricut maker machine should not be a new experience for you by now. However, it would be best if you kept an open mind to new updates. Cricut always gives its users many options to choose from, so try as much as possible to carry out extensive research about their products, materials, and subscriptions.

At this stage, we can both agree that Cricut offers a whole lot more than it requires. Do not give up trying to learn how to cut on Cricut machines. Although it might be a little frustrating getting design right sometimes, keep striving to attain perfection. You'll become professional in no time and probably start teaching other people how to use it.

Cricut machines are getting more popular every day. A lot of people have a preference for Cricut machines for many reasons. User-friendliness is one of the primary reasons that people choose Cricut machines to do their cutting job. It's easy to use and also easy to learn if you have the right resources. Almost anyone can set up a Cricut machine because it is not too complicated. All that a new user has to do is follow the straightforward instructions that come with the box.

There are so many amazing things that you can do with a Cricut maker machine. This book is only the beginning of what your creativity can do if you work with the Cricut machine. There are only new and better updates to the device, so now is the best time to get one and get in the door to understand what all it can do for you. We hope that the information we have provided you on what materials you can use with the machine, how to get your first project started, and all the project ideas are the tools you need to achieve the goals you have with the Cricut maker machine.

Keep this book handy as you start out working with your Cricut maker machine so that you always have a quick reference guide with you. This is an excellent way for you to get to know the device and not waste any time or material when you are just starting. It would help if you were well equipped to make all of your dreams' projects, and you are well on your way to impressing your friends and family with your newly acquired skill of homemade gifts and décor. It would help if you also took the time to consider selling your projects to make a profit. You can have an excellent side business in no time that can help you pay for the machine and the materials you are using and put some extra money in your pocket to pay your bills or get additional holiday gifts. There are many bonuses to getting a Cricut maker machine, and we hope you have the opportunity to discover them all.

If at any point you get stumped on how to use your machine or are wondering what materials you should use, reference the previous chapters or visit cricut.com for help. Understanding and reviewing your Cricut maker's foundations is wise to make sure you are building on your skills with a solid foundation of knowledge. From there, your creativity can blossom, and the sky is the limit for what you can create. So now, stop reading and start doing! Make your first t-shirt design or hanging planter, and enjoy your creations.

I hope that you enjoyed this book and learned a lot!

Thank you //

www.ingramcontent.com/pod-product-compliance
Lightning Source LLC
Chambersburg PA
CBHW080304030726
47593CB00009B/2631

9 781801 925204